The Glorious Journey
to God

Selections From Sacred Scriptures
on the Afterlife

Compiled by
Hushidar Motlagh, Ed.D.

The Glorious Journey to God

Holy Bible, New International Version (NIV)
Copyright © 1973, 1978, 1984. International Bible Society.
Used by permission of Zondervan Bible Publishers.

ISBN 0-937661-02-3
Library of Congress Catalog Card Number: 94-76944

*Dedicated to the Memory of
My Parents*

Contents

Part II
Selections From the
Writings of the Báb

Part III
Selections From Written And Spoken Words of 'Abdu'l-Bahá

Part IV
Prayers

Part V
Selections From the Qur'án

Various Teachings of the Qur'án
About an Afterlife

Return to God

Descriptions of Heaven
And Hell

Levels of Heaven and Hell

A Comparison Between Earthly Life and Heavenly

Part VI
Selections From
the New Testament

Part VII
Selections From
the Old Testament

Preface

- *Is death the door to a new life?*
- *Do hell and heaven really exist?*
- *What is the next world like?*
- *What does "hell-fire" mean?*
- *How glorious is paradise?*
- *Can we communicate with the departed?*
- *Are there opportunities to evolve after death?*
- *Can we meet our loved ones in the next world?*
- *What happens to infants who die?*
- *What is the purpose of this life?*
- *How can we prepare here for the hereafter?*
- *What are the proofs of an afterlife?*

These are some of the questions addressed in this book.

Death is always an occasion for grief, but should not be for gloom. Behind the clouds lies a dazzling beauty and celestial splendor beyond all description. One reason God conceals the glories of paradise is to help us enjoy the glories of this planet. Awareness of the immortal beauty of the hereafter would prevent us from pursuing our purpose here. Would it be possible to see the majestic splendor of the sun but live by the light of a candle?

Such is the station ordained for the true believer that if to an extent smaller than a needle's eye the glory of that station were to be unveiled to mankind, every beholder would be consumed away in his longing to attain it. For this reason it hath been decreed that in this earthly life the full measure of the glory of his own station should remain concealed from the eyes of such a believer. If the veil be lifted, and the full glory of the station of those who have turned wholly towards God, and in their love for Him renounced the world, be made manifest, the entire creation would be dumbfounded.[1]   Bahá'u'lláh

All sacred scriptures have testified to another life beyond this one, and little by little they have lifted the veil of mystery. Yet because of people's lack of receptivity and readiness, God's Messengers have kept many mysteries undisclosed:

> Close up and seal the words of the scroll until the time of the end.   Daniel 12:4

Sacred scriptures have prophesied that in due time "the scroll shall be unrolled," the seal broken, and the mysteries made manifest:

> ...the Ancient of Days [the Redeemer of our age] took his seat...and the books were opened.   Daniel 7:9

> The leaves of the Book [scroll] shall be unrolled...
>   Muhammad (Qur'án 81:10)

> I have much more to say to you, more than you can now bear. But when he, the Spirit of truth, comes, he will guide you into all truth [you are ready to hear].
>   Christ (John 16:12-13)

> ...wait till the Lord comes. He will bring to light what is hidden in darkness.   I Corinthians 4:5

Bahá'ís believe that the prophecies pointing to the disclosure of new knowledge and truth have been fulfilled by the Báb, Bahá'u'lláh, and 'Abdu'l-Bahá—the central figures of the Bahá'í Faith.

> Every hidden thing hath been brought to light by the virtue of the Will of the Supreme Ordainer...[2]   Bahá'u'lláh

The quotations offered here present convincing evidence of the fulfillment of the prophecies, of the outpouring of heavenly knowledge by God's latest revelation to humankind. Many of the mysteries that had been kept secret for thousands of years are disclosed in Bahá'í scriptures with astonishing clarity.

This compilation also includes quotations from the scriptures of three other religions: Judaism, Christianity, and Islam. Since Bahá'ís acknowledge the divine origin of all great faiths, they treat all sacred scriptures with the same reverence as their own. This compilation, perhaps the first of its kind, is the fruit of such a belief. The quotations clearly show the oneness of all faiths and their single source.

The order of the selections is from the most recent religion to the most ancient. This arrangement is helpful because as we go back in time the degree of clarity in sacred scriptures diminishes. By studying the Bahá'í references first, we are in a better position to understand the previous scriptures.

This book is not only about life after death but also life before death. The prime purpose of looking into the hereafter is to find and fulfill our purpose here. Bahá'u'lláh brings good news not only about our infinitely sublime and everlasting destiny in God's "many mansions," but also about our splendid future on this plane:

> The whole earth is now in a state of pregnancy. The day is approaching when it will have yielded its noblest fruits, when from it will have sprung forth the loftiest trees, the most enchanting blossoms, the most heavenly blessings.[3]
>
> Bahá'u'lláh

> All nations and kindreds will become a single nation. Religious and sectarian antagonism, the hostility of races and peoples, and differences among nations, will be eliminated. All men will adhere to one religion, will have one common faith, will be blended into one race, and become a single people. All will dwell in one common fatherland, which is the planet itself.[4]
>
> 'Abdu'l-Bahá

To balance the mystical with the practical, it seems fitting to offer a brief description of Bahá'u'lláh's teachings for a new world order and a new civilization on this war-torn and weary planet. The description may be helpful especially for those unfamiliar with the Bahá'í teachings.

Bahá'í Teachings For a
New World Order

The Bahá'í Faith is the second most widely spread religion in the world. It is the Faith promised in all sacred scriptures. It has come to unify all peoples and all religions and to spread hope and happiness to every heart and every home. It began in 1844 with the Báb (the Gate), the divinely inspired Herald of the new Faith. The Báb was imprisoned, exiled, and executed in 1850. In 1863, Bahá'u'lláh (Glory of God) declared that He was the One promised by the Báb and all great Messengers of the past. Both the Báb and Bahá'u'lláh are buried in Israel, not far from Nazareth.

Bahá'u'lláh wrote a hundred volumes. His works contain the divine plan for creating a world of peace and prosperity. He spoke with the same authority with which Jesus and all other great Messengers spoke. He was imprisoned and exiled for 40 years.

Bahá'u'lláh declares His message in the most definitive and emphatic terms. He invites all seekers and lovers of truth to investigate and embrace His Faith:

> The time foreordained unto the peoples and kindreds of the earth is now come. The promises of God, as recorded in the holy Scriptures, have all been fulfilled.[5]

> He, verily, is come with His Kingdom, and all the atoms cry aloud: "Lo! The Lord is come in His great majesty!"[6]

The ultimate goal of Bahá'u'lláh's divine plan is global unity. Ours is the age of the oneness of humanity. All nations, religions, and races must work together to overcome the obstacles that divide them. They must associate in a spirit of love and fellowship to create a new civilization based on justice, cooperation, peace, and concern for all humanity.

The first step in overcoming any obstacle or improving any condition is to expand one's perception. In the Bahá'í Faith this is called the *independent search for truth*.

To love truth for truth's sake is the principal part of human perfection in this world, and the seed-plot of all other virtues.

John Locke

As citizens of one planet, with one destiny, we must recognize that we are facing a new age with unparalleled crises and opportunities. We must reach beyond all the boundaries of our prevailing perceptions; our self-interests, untested beliefs and assumptions, our fear of the unfamiliar; and our submission to or tolerance for decayed and outmoded ideologies, such as nationalism, racism, sexism, and every other "ism" that places one segment of the human race apart from or above the others. We must also rise above the prevailing cynicism and apathy, the attitudes of "there is not much I can do" and "what will be will be."

Only the consciousness of a purpose that is mightier than any man and worthy of all men can fortify...the souls of men.

Walter Lippmann

We need to look with a new perspective on the world, religion, politics, economics, education, and our responsibilities as citizens of one planet. We need a new mode of thinking, a new vision inspired by our devotion to God and humanity with a desire to restore love and hope to the heart of the world.

Where there is no vision, the people perish... Proverbs 29:18

If we bring Bahá'u'lláh's vision of unity and peace to all the peoples of the planet, if we learn to communicate, to understand one another, to speak in one language, no goal, no dream can stand beyond our reach:

Then the Lord...said, 'Here they are one people with a single language, and now they have started to do this; henceforward nothing they have a mind to do will be beyond their reach.'

Genesis 11:6

Bahá'u'lláh not only gives us a grand vision of our divine role and destiny but the instrument through which we can make the vision a reality. To establish the New World Order and a new life for humankind, He presents these principles:

- *All great religions come from the same Source*. They unfold an ever-evolving truth; they reveal the divine wisdom progressively according to the needs and maturity of humankind. *Recognizing and respecting other great faiths is the most vital step toward unity and peace.*

- *The purpose of religion is to unify humanity*, to join people in love and harmony. But today religion is often a source of dissension and prejudice among the peoples of the world. This is the exact opposite of the true goal of religion. If a remedy intensifies the disease, it should be avoided.

- *Religion and science are perfect partners*. Their harmony must be recognized and their powers integrated. By decoding religious symbolism, the Bahá'í Faith demonstrates the unity—indeed the oneness—of these two vital forces in society.

- *Prejudice—racial, national, religious—must be uprooted*. Prejudice is a false perception that justifies selfish and egotistical desires and demands; it is a veil that distorts the truth and obscures reality. It blinds one's inner vision, and allows the ego to justify its selfish ends, descending to the depths of its desires. It is an impurity of the heart and the mind. Prejudice is so powerful, it can, by itself, stifle *any* achievement, prevent *any* progress, cause *any* conflict, lead to *any* crisis. Love of God is the most powerful weapon against it. This is the message the Bahá'ís are bringing back to the world. Prejudice cannot coexist with love and justice. Its prevalence is a proof of the loss of love in the heart of the humanity.

- *Sex discrimination must be abolished*. Equal opportunities and rights should be provided for both men and women. One's excellence depends on nobility of character, not on one's gender.

- *Universal education must become a reality*. It must enlighten and uplift the minds and hearts of all humanity. True knowledge expands and enriches human perception and vision.

- *Schools must teach both knowledge and nobility*. Education of children is the key to the success of the New World Order.

- *It is essential to establish universal peace*. Global war in our time means the virtual destruction of our planet and its people.

- ***Extremes of wealth and poverty must be eliminated,*** both through laws and through individuals' recognition of their spiritual responsibilities. As long as the masses of humanity cannot meet their basic needs, global unity and peace cannot be attained.

- ***Diversity among peoples and nations must be cherished and prized,*** for diversity enriches the world and enhances human perception. National customs and traditions should be preserved; diversity adorns and strengthens unity. The richness of an orchestra results from many instruments played in harmony.

- ***A universal auxiliary language must be adopted*** and learned throughout the planet. Communication is an essential prerequisite for understanding and peace. A family of nations whose members cannot talk to one another will not endure long.

- ***A global order must be established*** to regulate international relations. A planetary community cannot live by laws and regulations dictated by national self-interest. The time has come for establishing a global federation of nations.

- ***Our life's purpose is to know, to love, and to serve God by serving others.***

- ***We are in essence spiritual beings.*** To live in peace and contentment, to enjoy an abundant life, we must recognize our role in the grand cosmic plan of creation. Without knowledge of God and love of God no human being can reach his or her full spiritual potential. Growing without God is as impossible for humans as for a flower to bloom and flourish in darkness. If left on their own, human beings submit to their selfish needs and desires. When God enters their lives, He changes their perspective. The lesson they learn is this: serving one's self is great, but serving others is even greater. This perspective helps the individual to expand the small "circle of selfishness" to incorporate all human beings. Those who assume they can do without God only underestimate human potential.

Bahá'ís believe that the perception or mode of thinking that can save us from global conflict and war, the vision that can lead us to peace, prosperity, and contentment must include the recognition and realization of all the preceding principles.

This is the greatest day in human history, for all the prophecies have been fulfilled. This is the day of great rejoicing, for the Promised One has come:

Let the heavens rejoice, let the earth be glad; let the sea resound, and all that is in it; let the fields be jubilant, and everything in them. Then all the trees of the forest will sing for joy; they will sing before the Lord, for he comes, he comes to judge the earth.   Psalms 96:11-13
See also Psalms 97:1; 10-12; 98:1-9

In this Day a great festival is taking place in the Realm above; for whatsoever was promised in the sacred Scriptures hath been fulfilled. This is the Day of great rejoicing. It behoveth everyone to hasten towards the court of His nearness with exceeding joy, gladness, exultation and delight and to deliver himself from the fire of remoteness.[7]

Bahá'u'lláh

Know ye from what heights your Lord, the All Glorious, is calling?...Did ye but know it, ye would renounce the world, and would hasten with your whole hearts to the presence of the Well-Beloved...Thus have the showers of My bounty been poured down from the heaven of My loving-kindness, as a token of My grace, that ye may be of the thankful.[8]   Bahá'u'lláh

Sorrow not if, in these days and on this earthly plane, things contrary to your wishes have been ordained and manifested by God, for days of blissful joy, of heavenly delight, are assuredly in store for you. Worlds, holy and spiritually glorious, will be unveiled to your eyes. You are destined by Him, in this world and hereafter, to partake of their benefits, to share in their joys, and to obtain a portion of their sustaining grace. To each and every one of them you will, no doubt, attain.[9]   Bahá'u'lláh

Part I

Selections From the
Writings of Bahá'u'lláh

The State of the Soul
After This Life

And now concerning thy question regarding the soul of man
and its survival after death. Know thou of a truth that the
soul, after its separation from the body, will continue to
progress until it attaineth the presence of God, in a state and
condition which neither the revolution of ages and centuries,
nor the changes and chances of this world, can alter. It will
endure as long as the Kingdom of God, His sovereignty,
His dominion and power will endure. It will manifest the
signs of God and His attributes, and will reveal His loving
kindness and bounty. The movement of My Pen is stilled
when it attempteth to befittingly describe the loftiness and
glory of so exalted a station. The honor with which the
Hand of Mercy will invest the soul is such as no tongue can
adequately reveal, nor any other earthly agency describe.
Blessed is the soul which, at the hour of its separation from
the body, is sanctified from the vain imaginings of the peoples
of the world. Such a soul liveth and moveth in accordance
with the Will of its Creator, and entereth the all-highest
Paradise. The Maids of Heaven, inmates of the loftiest mansions,
will circle around it, and the Prophets of God and His chosen
ones will seek its companionship. With them that soul will
freely converse, and will recount unto them that which it hath
been made to endure in the path of God, the Lord of all
worlds. If any man be told that which hath been ordained
for such a soul in the worlds of God, the Lord of the
throne on high and of earth below, his whole being will
instantly blaze out in his great longing to attain that most
exalted, that sanctified and resplendent station....The nature
of the soul after death can never be described, nor is it
meet and permissible to reveal its whole character to the
eyes of men. The Prophets and Messengers of God have
been sent down for the sole purpose of guiding mankind to
the straight Path of Truth. The purpose underlying their
revelation hath been to educate all men, that they may, at
the hour of death, ascend, in the utmost purity and sanctity

and with absolute detachment, to the throne of the Most
High. The light which these souls radiate is responsible for
the progress of the world and the advancement of its peoples.
They are like unto leaven which leaveneth the world of
being, and constitute the animating force through which
the arts and wonders of the world are made manifest.
Through them the clouds rain their bounty upon men, and
the earth bringeth forth its fruits. All things must needs
have a cause, a motive power, an animating principle. These
souls and symbols of detachment have provided, and will
continue to provide, the supreme moving impulse in the
world of being. The world beyond is as different from this
world as this world is different from that of the child while
still in the womb of its mother. When the soul attaineth the
Presence of God, it will assume the form that best befitteth
its immortality and is worthy of its celestial habitation. Such
an existence is a contingent and not an absolute existence,
inasmuch as the former is preceded by a cause, whilst the
latter is independent thereof. Absolute existence is strictly
confined to God, exalted be His glory. Well is it with them
that apprehend this truth. Wert thou to ponder in thine
heart the behavior of the Prophets of God thou wouldst
assuredly and readily testify that there must needs be other
worlds besides this world. The majority of the truly wise and
learned have, throughout the ages, as it hath been recorded
by the Pen of Glory in the Tablet of Wisdom, borne witness to
the truth of that which the holy Writ of God hath revealed.
Even the materialists have testified in their writings to the
wisdom of these divinely-appointed Messengers, and have
regarded the references made by the Prophets to Paradise,
to hell fire, to future reward and punishment, to have been
actuated by a desire to educate and uplift the souls of men.
Consider, therefore, how the generality of mankind, whatever
their beliefs or theories, have recognized the excellence,
and admitted the superiority, of these Prophets of God.
These Gems of Detachment are acclaimed by some as the
embodiments of wisdom, while others believe them to be
the mouthpiece of God Himself. How could such Souls
have consented to surrender themselves unto their enemies

if they believed all the worlds of God to have been reduced to this earthly life? Would they have willingly suffered such afflictions and torments as no man hath ever experienced or witnessed?[1]

Consciousness After Death

And now concerning thy question whether human souls continue to be conscious one of another after their separation from the body. Know thou that the souls of the people of Bahá, who have entered and been established within the Crimson Ark, shall associate and commune intimately one with another, and shall be so closely associated in their lives, their aspirations, their aims and strivings as to be even as one soul. They are indeed the ones who are well-informed, who are keen-sighted, and who are endued with understanding. Thus hath it been decreed by Him Who is the All-Knowing, the All-Wise.

The people of Bahá, who are the inmates of the Ark of God, are, one and all, well aware of one another's state and condition, and are united in the bonds of intimacy and fellowship. Such a state, however, must depend upon their faith and their conduct. They that are of the same grade and station are fully aware of one another's capacity, character, accomplishments and merits. They that are of a lower grade, however, are incapable of comprehending adequately the station, or of estimating the merits, of those that rank above them. Each shall receive his share from thy Lord. Blessed is the man that hath turned his face towards God, and walked steadfastly in His love, until his soul hath winged its flight unto God, the Sovereign Lord of all, the Most Powerful, the Ever-Forgiving, the All-Merciful.

The souls of the infidels, however, shall—and to this I bear witness—when breathing their last be made aware of the good things that have escaped them, and shall bemoan their plight, and shall humble themselves before God. They shall continue doing so after the separation of their souls from their bodies.

It is clear and evident that all men shall, after their physical death, estimate the worth of their deeds, and realize all that their hands have wrought. I swear by the Day Star that shineth above the horizon of Divine power! They that are the followers of the one true God shall, the moment they depart out of this life, experience such joy and gladness as would be impossible to describe, while they that live in error shall be seized with such fear and trembling, and shall be filled with such consternation, as nothing can exceed. Well is it with him that hath quaffed the choice and incorruptible wine of faith through the gracious favor and the manifold bounties of Him Who is the Lord of all Faiths....[2]

The Worlds of God

As to thy question concerning the worlds of God. Know thou of a truth that the worlds of God are countless in their number, and infinite in their range. None can reckon or comprehend them except God, the All-Knowing, the All-Wise. Consider thy state when asleep. Verily, I say, this phenomenon is the most mysterious of the signs of God amongst men, were they to ponder it in their hearts. Behold how the thing which thou hast seen in thy dream is, after a considerable lapse of time, fully realized. Had the world in which thou didst find thyself in thy dream been identical with the world in which thou livest, it would have been necessary for the event occurring in that dream to have transpired in this world at the very moment of its occurrence. Were it so, you yourself would have borne witness unto it. This being not the case, however, it must necessarily follow that the world in which thou livest is different and apart from that which thou hast experienced in thy dream. This latter world hath neither beginning nor end. It would be true if thou wert to contend that this same world is, as decreed by the All-Glorious and Almighty God, within thy proper self and is wrapped up within thee. It would equally be true to maintain that thy spirit, having transcended the limitations of sleep and having stripped itself of all earthly attachment, hath, by the act of God, been made to traverse a realm which lieth hidden in the innermost reality of this world. Verily I say, the creation of God embraceth worlds besides this world, and creatures apart from these creatures. In each of these worlds He hath ordained things which none can search except Himself, the All-Searching, the All-Wise. Do thou meditate on that which We have revealed unto thee, that thou mayest discover the purpose of God, thy Lord, and the Lord of all worlds. In these words the mysteries of Divine Wisdom have been treasured. We have refrained from dwelling upon this theme owing to the sorrow that hath encompassed Us from the actions of them that have been created through Our words, if ye be of them that will hearken unto Our Voice.[3]

The Nature of the Soul

Thou hast asked Me concerning the nature of the soul. Know, verily, that the soul is a sign of God, a heavenly gem whose reality the most learned of men hath failed to grasp, and whose mystery no mind, however acute, can ever hope to unravel. It is the first among all created things to declare the excellence of its Creator, the first to recognize His glory, to cleave to His truth, and to bow down in adoration before Him. If it be faithful to God, it will reflect His light, and will, eventually, return unto Him. If it fail, however, in its allegiance to its Creator, it will become a victim to self and passion, and will, in the end, sink in their depths.

Whoso hath, in this Day, refused to allow the doubts and fancies of men to turn him away from Him Who is the Eternal Truth, and hath not suffered the tumult provoked by the ecclesiastical and secular authorities to deter him from recognizing His Message, such a man will be regarded by God, the Lord of all men, as one of His mighty signs, and will be numbered among them whose names have been inscribed by the Pen of the Most High in His Book. Blessed is he that hath recognized the true stature of such a soul, that hath acknowledged its station, and discovered its virtues.

Much hath been written in the books of old concerning the various stages in the development of the soul, such as concupiscence, irascibility, inspiration, benevolence, contentment, Divine good-pleasure, and the like; the Pen of the Most High, however, is disinclined to dwell upon them. Every soul that walketh humbly with its God, in this Day, and cleaveth unto Him, shall find itself invested with the honor and glory of all goodly names and stations.

When man is asleep, his soul can, in no wise, be said to have been inherently affected by any external object. It is not susceptible of any change in its original state or character. Any variation in its functions is to be ascribed to external causes. It is to these external influences that any variations in its environment, its understanding, and perception should be attributed.

Consider the human eye. Though it hath the faculty of perceiving all created things, yet the slightest impediment may so obstruct its vision as to deprive it of the power of discerning any object whatsoever. Magnified be the name of Him Who hath created, and is the Cause of, these causes, Who hath ordained that every change and variation in the world of being be made dependent upon them. Every created thing in the whole universe is but a door leading into His knowledge, a sign of His sovereignty, a revelation of His names, a symbol of His majesty, a token of His power, a means of admittance into His straight Path....

Verily I say, the human soul is, in its essence, one of the signs of God, a mystery among His mysteries. It is one of the mighty signs of the Almighty, the harbinger that proclaimeth the reality of all the worlds of God. Within it lieth concealed that which the world is now utterly incapable of apprehending. Ponder in thine heart the revelation of the Soul of God that pervadeth all His Laws, and contrast it with that base and appetitive nature that hath rebelled against Him, that forbiddeth men to turn unto the Lord of Names, and impelleth them to walk after their lusts and wickedness. Such a soul hath, in truth, wandered far in the path of error....

Thou hast, moreover, asked Me concerning the state of the soul after its separation from the body. Know thou, of a truth, that if the soul of man hath walked in the ways of God, it will, assuredly, return and be gathered to the glory of the Beloved. By the righteousness of God! It shall attain a station such as no pen can depict, or tongue describe. The soul that hath remained faithful to the Cause of God, and stood unwaveringly firm in His Path shall, after his ascension, be possessed of such power that all the worlds which the Almighty hath created can benefit through him. Such a soul provideth, at the bidding of the Ideal King and Divine Educator, the pure leaven that leaveneth the world of being, and furnisheth the power through which the arts and wonders of the world are made manifest. Consider how meal needeth leaven to be leavened with. Those souls that are the symbols of detachment are the leaven of the world. Meditate on this, and be of the thankful.

In several of Our Tablets We have referred to this theme, and have set forth the various stages in the development of the soul. Verily I say, the human soul is exalted above all egress and regress. It is still, and yet it soareth; it moveth, and yet it is still. It is, in itself, a testimony that beareth witness to the existence of a world that is contingent, as well as to the reality of a world that hath neither beginning nor end. Behold how the dream thou hast dreamed is, after the lapse of many years, re-enacted before thine eyes. Consider how strange is the mystery of the world that appeareth to thee in thy dream. Ponder in thine heart upon the unsearchable wisdom of God, and meditate on its manifold revelations....

Witness the wondrous evidences of God's handiwork, and reflect upon its range and character. He Who is the Seal of the Prophets hath said: "Increase my wonder and amazement at Thee, O God!"

As to thy question whether the physical world is subject to any limitations, know thou that the comprehension of this matter dependeth upon the observer himself. In one sense, it is limited; in another, it is exalted beyond all limitations. The one true God hath everlastingly existed, and will everlastingly continue to exist. His creation, likewise, hath had no beginning, and will have no end. All that is created, however, is preceded by a cause. This fact, in itself, establisheth, beyond the shadow of a doubt, the unity of the Creator.[4]

Man's Unique Distinction

Having created the world and all that liveth and moveth therein, He, through the direct operation of His unconstrained and sovereign Will, chose to confer upon man the unique distinction and capacity to know Him and to love Him—a capacity that must needs be regarded as the generating impulse and the primary purpose underlying the whole of creation....Upon the inmost reality of each and every created thing He hath shed the light of one of His names, and made it a recipient of the glory of one of His attributes. Upon the reality of man, however, He hath focused the radiance of all of His names and attributes, and made it a mirror of His own Self. Alone of all created things man hath been singled out for so great a favor, so enduring a bounty.[5]

Distinctions Bestowed Upon Man

All-praise and glory be to God Who, through the power of His might, hath delivered His creation from the nakedness of non-existence, and clothed it with the mantle of life. From among all created things He hath singled out for His special favor the pure, the gem-like reality of man, and invested it with a unique capacity of knowing Him and of reflecting the greatness of His glory.

This twofold distinction conferred upon him hath cleansed away from his heart the rust of every vain desire, and made him worthy of the vesture with which his Creator hath deigned to clothe him. It hath served to rescue his soul from the wretchedness of ignorance.

This robe with which the body and soul of man hath been adorned is the very foundation of his well-being and development. Oh, how blessed the day when, aided by the grace and might of the one true God, man will have freed himself from the bondage and corruption of the world and all that is therein, and will have attained unto true and abiding rest beneath the shadow of the Tree of Knowledge![6]

The Soul's Independence of Physical Infirmities

Thou hast asked Me whether man, as apart from the Prophets of God and His chosen ones, will retain, after his physical death, the self-same individuality, personality, consciousness, and understanding that characterize his life in this world. If this should be the case, how is it, thou hast observed, that whereas such slight injuries to his mental faculties as fainting and severe illness deprive him of his understanding and consciousness, his death, which must involve the decomposition of his body and the dissolution of its elements, is powerless to destroy that understanding and extinguish that consciousness? How can any one imagine that man's consciousness and personality will be maintained, when the very instruments necessary to their existence and function will have completely disintegrated?

Know thou that the soul of man is exalted above, and is independent of all infirmities of body or mind. That a sick person showeth signs of weakness is due to the hindrances that interpose themselves between his soul and his body, for the soul itself remaineth unaffected by any bodily ailments. Consider the light of the lamp. Though an external object may interfere with its radiance, the light itself continueth to shine with undiminished power. In like manner, every malady afflicting the body of man is an impediment that preventeth the soul from manifesting its inherent might and power. When it leaveth the body, however, it will evince such ascendancy, and reveal such influence as no force on earth can equal. Every pure, every refined and sanctified soul will be endowed with tremendous power, and shall rejoice with exceeding gladness.

Consider the lamp which is hidden under a bushel. Though its light be shining, yet its radiance is concealed from men. Likewise, consider the sun which hath been obscured by the clouds. Observe how its splendor appeareth to have diminished, when in reality the source of that light hath remained unchanged. The soul of man should be likened unto this sun, and all things on earth should be regarded as his body. So long as no external impediment interveneth between them, the body will, in its entirety, continue to reflect the light of the soul, and to be sustained by its power. As soon as, however, a veil interposeth itself between them, the brightness of that light seemeth to lessen.

Consider again the sun when it is completely hidden behind the clouds. Though the earth is still illumined with its light, yet the measure of light which it receiveth is considerably reduced. Not until the clouds have dispersed, can the sun shine again in the plenitude of its glory. Neither the presence of the cloud nor its absence can, in any way, affect the inherent splendor of the sun. The soul of man is the sun by which his body is illumined, and from which it draweth its sustenance, and should be so regarded.

Consider, moreover, how the fruit, ere it is formed, lieth potentially within the tree. Were the tree to be cut into pieces, no sign nor any part of the fruit, however small, could be detected. When it appeareth, however, it manifesteth itself, as thou hast observed, in its wondrous beauty and glorious perfection. Certain fruits, indeed, attain their fullest development only after being severed from the tree.[7]

The Dependence of the Body on the Rational Faculty

Consider the rational faculty with which God hath endowed the essence of man. Examine thine own self, and behold how thy motion and stillness, thy will and purpose, thy sight and hearing, thy sense of smell and power of speech, and whatever else is related to, or transcendeth, thy physical senses or spiritual perceptions, all proceed from, and owe their existence to, this same faculty. So closely are they related unto it, that if in less than the twinkling of an eye its relationship to the human body be severed, each and every one of these senses will cease immediately to exercise its function, and will be deprived of the power to manifest the evidences of its activity. It is indubitably clear and evident that each of these afore-mentioned instruments has depended, and will ever continue to depend, for its proper functioning on this rational faculty, which should be regarded as a sign of the revelation of Him Who is the sovereign Lord of all. Through its manifestation all these names and attributes have been revealed, and by the suspension of its action they are all destroyed and perish.

It would be wholly untrue to maintain that this faculty is the same as the power of vision, inasmuch as the power of vision is derived from it and acteth in dependence upon it. It would, likewise, be idle to contend that this faculty can be identified with the sense of hearing, as the sense of hearing receiveth from the rational faculty the requisite energy for performing its functions.

This same relationship bindeth this faculty with whatsoever hath been the recipient of these names and attributes within the human temple. These diverse names and revealed attributes have been generated through the agency of this sign of God. Immeasurably exalted is this sign, in its essence and reality, above all such names and attributes. Nay, all else besides it will, when compared with its glory, fade into utter nothingness and become a thing forgotten.

Wert thou to ponder in thine heart, from now until the end that hath no end, and with all the concentrated intelligence and understanding which the greatest minds have attained in the past or will attain in the future, this divinely ordained and subtle Reality, this sign of the revelation of the All-Abiding, All-Glorious God, thou wilt fail to comprehend its mystery or to appraise its virtue.[8]

The World of Dreams as Evidence of an Afterlife

One of the created phenomena is the dream. Behold how many secrets are deposited therein, how many wisdoms treasured up, how many worlds concealed. Observe, how thou art asleep in a dwelling, and its doors are barred; on a sudden thou findest thyself in a far-off city, which thou enterest without moving thy feet or wearying thy body; without using thine eyes, thou seest; without taxing thine ears, thou hearest; without a tongue, thou speakest. And perchance when ten years are gone, thou wilt witness in the outer world the very things thou hast dreamed tonight.

Now there are many wisdoms to ponder in the dream...

First, what is this world, where without eye and ear and hand and tongue a man puts all of these to use? Second, how is it that in the outer world thou seest today the effect of a dream, when thou didst vision it in the world of sleep some ten years past? Consider the difference between these two worlds and the mysteries which they conceal, that thou mayest attain to divine confirmations and heavenly discoveries and enter the regions of holiness.

God, the Exalted, hath placed these signs in men, to the end that philosophers may not deny the mysteries of the life beyond nor belittle that which hath been promised them.[9]

Man's Creation

And now, concerning thy question regarding the creation of man. Know thou that all men have been created in the nature made by God, the Guardian, the Self-Subsisting. Unto each one hath been prescribed a pre-ordained measure, as decreed in God's mighty and guarded Tablets. All that which ye potentially possess can, however, be manifested only as a result of your own volition. Your own acts testify to this truth.[10]

The Supreme Destiny of the True Believer

It is clear and evident that when the veils that conceal the realities of the manifestations of the Names and Attributes of God, nay of all created things visible or invisible, have been rent asunder, nothing except the Sign of God will remain—a sign which He, Himself, hath placed within these realities. This sign will endure as long as is the wish of the Lord thy God, the Lord of the heavens and of the earth. If such be the blessings conferred on all created things, how superior must be the destiny of the true believer, whose existence and life are to be regarded as the originating purpose of all creation. Just as the conception of faith hath existed from the beginning that hath no beginning, and will endure till the end that hath no end, in like manner will the true believer eternally live and endure. His spirit will everlastingly circle round the Will of God. He will last as long as God, Himself, will last. He is revealed through the Revelation of God, and is hidden at His bidding. It is evident that the loftiest mansions in the Realm of Immortality have been ordained as the habitation of them that have truly believed in God and in His signs. Death can never invade that holy seat. Thus have We entrusted thee with the signs of Thy Lord, that thou mayest persevere in thy love for Him, and be of them that comprehend this truth.[11]

Man's Exalted Station

Great and blessed is this Day—the Day in which all that lay latent in man hath been and will be made manifest. Lofty is the station of man, were he to hold fast to righteousness and truth and to remain firm and steadfast in the Cause. In the eyes of the All-Merciful a true man appeareth even as a firmament; its sun and moon are his sight and hearing, and his shining and resplendent character its stars. His is the loftiest station, and his influence educateth the world of being.[12]

The Noblest of All Creatures

Whatever is in the heavens and whatever is on the earth is a direct evidence of the revelation within it of the attributes and names of God, inasmuch as within every atom are enshrined the signs that bear eloquent testimony to the revelation of that Most Great Light. Methinks, but for the potency of that revelation, no being could ever exist. How resplendent the luminaries of knowledge that shine in an atom, and how vast the oceans of wisdom that surge within a drop! To a supreme degree is this true of man, who, among all created things, hath been invested with the robe of such gifts, and hath been singled out for the glory of such distinction. For in him are potentially revealed all the attributes and names of God to a degree that no other created being hath excelled or surpassed. All these names and attributes are applicable to him. Even as He hath said: "Man is My mystery, and I am his mystery." Manifold are the verses that have been repeatedly revealed in all the Heavenly Books and the Holy Scriptures, expressive of this most subtle and lofty theme. Even as He hath revealed: "We will surely show them Our signs in the world and within themselves." Again He saith: "And also in your own selves: will ye not, then, behold the signs of God?" And yet again He revealeth: "And be ye not like those who forget God, and whom He hath therefore caused to forget their own selves." In this connection, He Who is the eternal King—may the souls of all that dwell within the mystic Tabernacle be a sacrifice unto Him—hath spoken: "He hath known God who hath known himself."

...From that which hath been said it becometh evident that all things, in their inmost reality, testify to the revelation of the names and attributes of God within them. Each according to its capacity, indicateth, and is expressive of, the knowledge of God. So potent and universal is this revelation, that it hath encompassed all things visible and invisible. Thus hath He revealed: "Hath aught else save Thee a power of revelation which is not possessed by Thee, that it could have manifested Thee? Blind is the eye which doth not perceive Thee." Likewise hath the eternal King spoken: "No thing have I perceived, except that I perceived God within it, God before it, or God after it." Also in the tradition of Kumayl it is written: "Behold, a light hath shone forth out of the morn of eternity, and lo, its waves have penetrated the inmost reality of all men." Man, the noblest and most perfect of all created things, excelleth them all in the intensity of this revelation, and is a fuller expression of its glory. And of all men, the most accomplished, the most distinguished, and the most excellent are the Manifestations of the Sun of Truth. Nay, all else besides these Manifestations, live by the operation of their Will, and move and have their being through the out-pourings of their grace.[13]

Trapped by Desire

Ye are even as the bird which soareth, with the full force of its mighty wings and with complete and joyous confidence, through the immensity of the heavens, until, impelled to satisfy its hunger, it turneth longingly to the water and clay of the earth below it, and, having been entrapped in the mesh of its desire, findeth itself impotent to resume its flight to the realms whence it came. Powerless to shake off the burden weighing on its sullied wings, that bird, hitherto an inmate of the heavens, is now forced to seek a dwelling-place upon the dust.[14]

The Station of True Believers

As to those that have tasted of the fruit of man's earthly existence, which is the recognition of the one true God, exalted be His glory, their life hereafter is such as We are unable to describe. The knowledge thereof is with God, alone, the Lord of all worlds.[15]

Days of Blissful Joy

O My servants! Sorrow not if, in these days and on this earthly plane, things contrary to your wishes have been ordained and manifested by God, for days of blissful joy, of heavenly delight, are assuredly in store for you. Worlds, holy and spiritually glorious, will be unveiled to your eyes. You are destined by Him, in this world and hereafter, to partake of their benefits, to share in their joys, and to obtain a portion of their sustaining grace. To each and every one of them you will, no doubt, attain.[16]

A Glimpse of Paradise

As to Paradise: It is a reality and there can be no doubt about it, and now in this world it is realized through love of Me and My good-pleasure. Whosoever attaineth unto it God will aid him in this world below, and after death He will enable him to gain admittance into Paradise whose vastness is as that of heaven and earth. Therein the Maids of glory and holiness will wait upon him in the daytime and in the night season, while the daystar of the unfading beauty of his Lord will at all times shed its radiance upon him and he will shine so brightly that no one shall bear to gaze at him. Such is the dispensation of Providence, yet the people are shut out by a grievous veil. Likewise apprehend thou the nature of hell-fire and be of them that truly believe. For every act performed there shall be a recompense according to the estimate of God, and unto this the very ordinances and prohibitions prescribed by the Almighty amply bear witness. For surely if deeds were not rewarded and yielded no fruit, then the Cause of God—exalted is He—would prove futile. Immeasurably high is He exalted above such blasphemies! However, unto them that are rid of all attachments a deed is, verily, its own reward. Were We to enlarge upon this theme numerous Tablets would need to be written.[17]

Being Born Again

Even as Jesus said: "Ye must be born again."* Again He saith: "Except a man be born of water and of the Spirit, he cannot enter into the Kingdom of God. That which is born of the flesh is flesh; and that which is born of the Spirit is spirit."✦ The purport of these words is that whosoever in every dispensation is born of the Spirit and is quickened by the breath of the Manifestation of Holiness, he verily is of those that have attained unto "life" and "resurrection" and have entered into the "paradise" of the love of God. And whosoever is not of them, is condemned to "death" and "deprivation," to the "fire" of unbelief, and to the "wrath" of God. In all the scriptures, the books and chronicles, the sentence of death, of fire, of blindness, of want of understanding and hearing, hath been pronounced against those whose lips have tasted not the ethereal cup of true knowledge, and whose hearts have been deprived of the grace of the holy Spirit in their day.[18]

---

*John 3:7.
✦John 3:5-6.

The Hidden Glory

Persevere thou conscientiously in the service of the Cause and, through the power of the Name of thy Lord, the Possessor of all things visible and invisible, preserve the station conferred upon thee. I swear by the righteousness of God! Were anyone apprised of that which is veiled from the eyes of men, he would become so enraptured as to wing his flight unto God, the Lord of all that hath been and shall be.[19]

O Maid of Heaven

Say: Step out of Thy holy chamber, O Maid of Heaven, inmate of the Exalted Paradise! Drape thyself in whatever manner pleaseth Thee in the silken Vesture of Immortality, and put on, in the name of the All-Glorious, the broidered Robe of Light. Hear, then, the sweet, the wondrous accent of the Voice that cometh from the Throne of Thy Lord, the Inaccessible, the Most High. Unveil Thy face, and manifest the beauty of the black-eyed Damsel, and suffer not the servants of God to be deprived of the light of Thy shining countenance. Grieve not if Thou hearest the sighs of the dwellers of the earth, or the voice of the lamentation of the denizens of heaven. Leave them to perish on the dust of extinction. Let them be reduced to nothingness, inasmuch as the flame of hatred hath been kindled within their breasts. Intone, then, before the face of the peoples of earth and heaven, and in a most melodious voice, the anthem of praise, for a remembrance of Him Who is the King of the names and attributes of God. Thus have We decreed Thy destiny. Well able are We to achieve Our purpose.

Beware that Thou divest not Thyself, Thou Who art the Essence of Purity, of Thy robe of effulgent glory. Nay, enrich Thyself increasingly, in the kingdom of creation, with the incorruptible vestures of Thy God, that the beauteous image of the Almighty may be reflected through Thee in all created things and the grace of Thy Lord be infused in the plenitude of its power into the entire creation.

If Thou smellest from any one the smell of the love of Thy Lord, offer up Thyself for him, for We have created Thee to this end, and have covenanted with Thee, from time immemorial, and in the presence of the congregation of Our well-favored ones, for this very purpose. Be not impatient if the blind in heart hurl down the shafts of their idle fancies upon Thee. Leave them to themselves, for they follow the promptings of the evil ones.

Cry out before the gaze of the dwellers of heaven and of earth: I am the Maid of Heaven, the Offspring begotten by the Spirit of Bahá. My habitation is the Mansion of His Name, the All-Glorious. Before the Concourse on high I was adorned with the ornament of His names. I was wrapt within the veil of all inviolable security, and lay hidden from the eyes of men. Methinks that I heard a Voice of divine and incomparable sweetness, proceeding from the right hand of the God of Mercy, and lo, the whole Paradise stirred and trembled before Me, in its longing to hear its accents, and gaze on the beauty of Him that uttered them.[20]

The Meaning of "Angels"

And now, concerning His words: "And He shall send His angels...." By "angels" is meant those who, reinforced by the power of the spirit, have consumed, with the fire of the love of God, all human traits and limitations, and have clothed themselves with the attributes of the most exalted Beings and of the Cherubim....

And now, inasmuch as these holy beings have sanctified themselves from every human limitation, have become endowed with the attributes of the spiritual, and have been adorned with the noble traits of the blessed, they therefore have been designated as "angels."[21]

The Fire of Remoteness From God

Whoso hath failed to recognize Him will have condemned himself to the misery of remoteness, a remoteness which is naught but utter nothingness and the essence of the nethermost fire. Such will be his fate, though to outward seeming he may occupy the earth's loftiest seats and be established upon its most exalted throne.[22]

The Day of Reckoning

Erelong shall your days pass away, as shall pass away the days of those who now, with flagrant pride, vaunt themselves over their neighbor. Soon shall ye be gathered together in the presence of God, and shall be asked of your doings, and shall be repaid for what your hands have wrought, and wretched the abode of the wicked doers!

By God! Wert thou to realize what thou hast done, thou wouldst surely weep sore over thyself, and wouldst flee for refuge to God, and wouldst pine away and mourn all the days of thy life, till God will have forgiven thee, for He, verily, is the Most Generous, the All-Bountiful. Thou wilt, however, persist, till the hour of thy death, in thy heedlessness, inasmuch as thou hast, with all thine heart, thy soul and inmost being, busied thyself with the vanities of the world. Thou shalt, after thy departure, discover what We have revealed unto thee, and shalt find all thy doings recorded in the Book wherein the works of all them that dwell on earth, be they greater or less than the weight of an atom, are noted down. Heed, therefore, My counsel, and hearken thou, with the hearing of thine heart, unto My speech, and be not careless of My words, nor be of them that reject My truth. Glory not in the things that have been given thee. Set before thine eyes what hath been revealed in the Book of God, the Help in Peril, the All-Glorious: "And when they had forgotten their warnings, We set open to thee...and to thy like the gates of this earth and the ornaments thereof. Wait thou, therefore, for what hath been promised in the latter part of this holy verse, for this is a promise from Him Who is the Almighty, the All-Wise—a promise that will not prove untrue.[23]

Selections From the Hidden Words

O SON OF MAN!
Thou art My dominion and My dominion perisheth not, wherefore fearest thou thy perishing? Thou art My light and My light shall never be extinguished, why dost thou dread extinction? Thou art My glory and My glory fadeth not; thou art My robe and My robe shall never be outworn. Abide then in thy love for Me, that thou mayest find Me in the realm of glory.[24]

O SON OF THE SUPREME!
I have made death a messenger of joy to thee. Wherefore dost thou grieve? I made the light to shed on thee its splendor. Why dost thou veil thyself therefrom?[25]

O SON OF MAN!
Ascend unto My heaven, that thou mayest obtain the joy of reunion, and from the chalice of imperishable glory quaff the peerless wine.[26]

O YE SONS OF SPIRIT!
Ye are My treasury, for in you I have treasured the pearls of My mysteries and the gems of My knowledge. Guard them from the strangers amidst My servants and from the ungodly amongst My people.[27]

O MY SERVANT!
Abandon not for that which perisheth an everlasting dominion, and cast not away celestial sovereignty for a worldly desire. This is the river of everlasting life that hath flowed from the well-spring of the pen of the merciful; well is it with them that drink![28]

O MY SERVANT!

Free thyself from the fetters of this world, and loose thy soul from the prison of self. Seize thy chance, for it will come to thee no more.[29]

O SON OF MY HANDMAID!

Didst thou behold immortal sovereignty, thou wouldst strive to pass from this fleeting world. But to conceal the one from thee and to reveal the other is a mystery which none but the pure in heart can comprehend.[30]

O COMPANION OF MY THRONE!

...Live then the days of thy life, that are less than a fleeting moment, with thy mind stainless, thy heart unsullied, thy thoughts pure, and thy nature sanctified, so that, free and content, thou mayest put away this mortal frame, and repair unto the mystic paradise and abide in the eternal kingdom for evermore.[31]

O SON OF WORLDLINESS!

Pleasant is the realm of being, wert thou to attain thereto; glorious is the domain of eternity, shouldst thou pass beyond the world of mortality; sweet is the holy ecstasy if thou drinkest of the mystic chalice from the hands of the celestial Youth. Shouldst thou attain this station, thou wouldst be freed from destruction and death, from toil and sin.[32]

O CHILDREN OF NEGLIGENCE!

Set not your affections on mortal sovereignty and rejoice not therein. Ye are even as the unwary bird that with full confidence warbleth upon the bough; till of a sudden the fowler Death throws it upon the dust, and the melody, the form and the color are gone, leaving not a trace. Wherefore take heed, O bondslaves of desire![33]

O SON OF BEING!

Thy Paradise is My love; thy heavenly home, reunion with Me. Enter therein and tarry not. This is that which hath been destined for thee in Our kingdom above and Our exalted dominion.[34]

O SON OF THE SUPREME!

To the eternal I call thee, yet thou dost seek that which perisheth. What hath made thee turn away from Our desire and seek thine own?[35]

O SON OF SPIRIT!

With the joyful tidings of light I hail thee: rejoice! To the court of holiness I summon thee; abide therein that thou mayest live in peace for evermore.[36]

O SON OF SPIRIT!

The spirit of holiness beareth unto thee the joyful tidings of reunion; wherefore dost thou grieve? The spirit of power confirmeth thee in His cause; why dost thou veil thyself? The light of His countenance doth lead thee; how canst thou go astray?[37]

O SON OF MAN!

Sorrow not save that thou art far from Us. Rejoice not save that thou art drawing near and returning unto Us.[38]

O SON OF MAN!

The light hath shone on thee from the horizon of the sacred Mount and the spirit of enlightenment hath breathed in the Sinai of thy heart. Wherefore, free thyself from the veils of idle fancies and enter into My court, that thou mayest be fit for everlasting life and worthy to meet Me. Thus may death not come upon thee, neither weariness nor trouble.[39]

O SON OF BOUNTY!

Out of the wastes of nothingness, with the clay of My command I made thee to appear, and have ordained for thy training every atom in existence and the essence of all created things. Thus, ere thou didst issue from thy mother's womb, I destined for thee two founts of gleaming milk, eyes to watch over thee, and hearts to love thee. Out of My loving-kindness, 'neath the shade of My mercy I nurtured thee, and guarded thee by the essence of My grace and favor. And My purpose in all this was that thou mightest attain My everlasting dominion and become worthy of My invisible bestowals. And yet heedless thou didst remain, and when fully grown, thou didst neglect all My bounties and occupied thyself with thine idle imaginings, in such wise that thou didst become wholly forgetful, and, turning away from the portals of the Friend didst abide within the courts of My enemy.[40]

O OFFSPRING OF DUST!
Be not content with the ease of a passing day, and deprive not thyself of everlasting rest. Barter not the garden of eternal delight for the dust-heap of a mortal world. Up from thy prison ascend unto the glorious meads above, and from thy mortal cage wing thy flight unto the paradise of the Placeless.[41]

O MY FRIEND!
Thou art the day-star of the heavens of My holiness, let not the defilement of the world eclipse thy splendor. Rend asunder the veil of heedlessness, that from behind the clouds thou mayest emerge resplendent and array all things with the apparel of life.[42]

Fate And Predestination

O thou who art the fruit of My Tree and the leaf thereof! On thee be My glory and My mercy. Let not thine heart grieve over what hath befallen thee. Wert thou to scan the pages of the Book of Life, thou wouldst, most certainly, discover that which would dissipate thy sorrows and dissolve thine anguish.

Know thou, O fruit of My Tree, that the decrees of the Sovereign Ordainer, as related to fate and predestination, are of two kinds. Both are to be obeyed and accepted. The one is irrevocable, the other is, as termed by men, impending. To the former all must unreservedly submit, inasmuch as it is fixed and settled. God, however, is able to alter or repeal it. As the harm that must result from such a change will be greater than if the decree had remained unaltered, all, therefore, should willingly acquiesce in what God hath willed and confidently abide by the same.

The decree that is impending, however, is such that prayer and entreaty can succeed in averting it.

God grant that thou who art the fruit of My Tree, and they that are associated with thee, may be shielded from its evil consequences.[43]

The Middle Way

Lament not in your hours of trial, neither rejoice therein; seek ye the Middle Way which is the remembrance of Me in your afflictions and reflection over that which may befall you in future. Thus informeth you, He Who is the Omniscient, He Who is Aware.[44]

On the Loss of a Son

On her be My blessings, and My mercy, and My praise, and My glory. I Myself shall atone for the loss of her son—a son who now dwelleth within the tabernacle of My majesty and glory, and whose face beameth with a light that envelopeth with its radiance the Maids of Heaven in their celestial chambers, and beyond them the inmates of My Paradise, and the denizens of the Cities of Holiness. Were any eye to gaze on his face, he would exclaim: "Lo, this is no other than a noble angel!"[45]

Deeds Recorded

Think not the deeds ye have committed have been blotted from My sight. By My beauty! All your doings hath My Pen graven with open characters upon tablets of chrysolite.[46]

Divine Assistance

Let not your hearts be perturbed, O people, when the glory
of My Presence is withdrawn, and the ocean of My utterance
is stilled. In My presence amongst you there is a wisdom,
and in My absence there is yet another, inscrutable to all but
God, the Incomparable, the All-Knowing. Verily, We behold
you from Our realm of glory, and shall aid whosoever will
arise for the triumph of Our Cause with the hosts of the
Concourse on high and a company of Our favored angels.[47]

Daily Reckoning

Set before thine eyes God's unerring Balance and, as one
standing in His Presence, weigh in that Balance thine actions
every day, every moment of thy life. Bring thyself to account
ere thou art summoned to a reckoning, on the Day when
no man shall have strength to stand for fear of God, the
Day when the hearts of the heedless ones shall be made to
tremble.[48]

The Final Reckoning

Ye will most certainly be called upon to answer for His trust
on the day when the Balance of Justice shall be set, the day
when unto every one shall be rendered his due, when the
doings of all men, be they rich or poor, shall be weighed.[49]

* * *

Ye, and all ye possess, shall pass away. Ye shall, most certainly,
return to God, and shall be called to account for your doings
in the presence of Him Who shall gather together the entire
creation...[50]

This Transitory Life

The world is continually proclaiming these words: Beware, I am evanescent, and so are all my outward appearances and colors. Take ye heed of the changes and chances contrived within me and be ye roused from your slumber. Nevertheless there is no discerning eye to see, nor is there a hearing ear to hearken.[51]

* * *

Beware lest the transitory things of human life withhold you from turning unto God, the True One. Ponder ye in your hearts the world and its conflicts and changes, so that ye may discern its merit and the station of those who have set their hearts upon it and have turned away from that which hath been sent down in Our Preserved Tablet.[52]

The Swiftly Passing Days

Night hath succeeded day, and day hath succeeded night, and the hours and moments of your lives have come and gone, and yet none of you hath, for one instant, consented to detach himself from that which perisheth. Bestir yourselves, that the brief moments that are still yours may not be dissipated and lost. Even as the swiftness of lightning your days shall pass, and your bodies shall be laid to rest beneath a canopy of dust. What can ye then achieve? How can ye atone for your past failure?[53]

The World As a Show

The world is but a show, vain and empty, a mere nothing, bearing the semblance of reality. Set not your affections upon it. Break not the bond that uniteth you with your

Creator, and be not of those that have erred and strayed
from His ways. Verily I say, the world is like the vapor in a
desert, which the thirsty dreameth to be water and striveth
after it with all his might, until when he cometh unto it, he
findeth it to be mere illusion.[54]

The Destiny of the Proud and Powerful

Exultest thou over the treasures thou dost possess, knowing
they shall perish? Rejoicest thou in that thou rulest a span
of earth, when the whole world, in the estimation of the
people of Bahá, is worth as much as the black in the eye of a
dead ant? Abandon it unto such as have set their affections
upon it, and turn thou unto Him Who is the Desire of the
world. Whither are gone the proud and their palaces? Gaze
thou into their tombs, that thou mayest profit by this example,
inasmuch as We made it a lesson unto every beholder. Were
the breezes of Revelation to seize thee, thou wouldst flee
the world, and turn unto the Kingdom, and wouldst expend
all thou possessest, that thou mayest draw nigh unto this
sublime Vision.[55]

Relying on God

The days of your life are far spent, O people, and your end
is fast approaching. Put away, therefore, the things ye have
devised and to which ye cleave, and take firm hold on the
precepts of God, that haply ye may attain that which He
hath purposed for you, and be of them that pursue a right
course. Delight not yourselves in the things of the world
and its vain ornaments, neither set your hopes on them. Let
your reliance be on the remembrance of God, the Most
Exalted, the Most Great. He will, erelong, bring to naught

all the things ye possess. Let Him be your fear, and forget not His covenant with you, and be not of them that are shut out as by a veil from Him.[56]

Choose the Love of God

The generations that have gone on before you—whither are they fled? And those round whom in life circled the fairest and the loveliest of the land, where now are they? Profit by their example, O people, and be not of them that are gone astray.

Others ere long will lay hands on what ye possess, and enter into your habitations. Incline your ears to My words, and be not numbered among the foolish.

For every one of you his paramount duty is to choose for himself that on which no other may infringe and none usurp from him. Such a thing—and to this the Almighty is My witness—is the love of God, could ye but perceive it.

Build ye for yourselves such houses as the rain and floods can never destroy, which shall protect you from the changes and chances of this life. This is the instruction of Him Whom the world hath wronged and forsaken.[57]

Earthly Treasure as Distraction

We see you rejoicing in that which ye have amassed for others and shutting out yourselves from the worlds which naught except My guarded Tablet can reckon. The treasures ye have laid up have drawn you far away from your ultimate objective. This ill beseemeth you, could ye but understand it. Wash from your hearts all earthly defilements, and hasten to enter the Kingdom of your Lord, the Creator of earth and heaven, Who caused the world to tremble and all its peoples to wail, except them that have renounced all things and clung to that which the Hidden Tablet hath ordained.[58]

Earthly Vanities Worthless

By the righteousness of God! The world and its vanities, and its glory, and whatever delights it can offer, are all, in the sight of God, as worthless as, nay, even more contemptible than, dust and ashes. Would that the hearts of men could comprehend it! Cleanse yourselves thoroughly, O people of Bahá, from the defilement of the world, and of all that pertaineth unto it. God Himself beareth Me witness. The things of the earth ill beseem you. Cast them away unto such as may desire them, and fasten your eyes upon this most holy and effulgent Vision.

That which beseemeth you is the love of God, and the love of Him Who is the Manifestation of His Essence, and the observance of whatsoever He chooseth to prescribe unto you, did ye but know it.[59]

Spiritual Life the True Life

Wert thou to attain to but a dewdrop of the crystal waters of divine knowledge, thou wouldst readily realize that true life is not the life of the flesh but the life of the spirit. For the life of the flesh is common to both men and animals, whereas the life of the spirit is possessed only by the pure in heart who have quaffed from the ocean of faith and partaken of the fruit of certitude. This life knoweth no death, and this existence is crowned by immortality. Even as it hath been said: "He who is a true believer liveth both in this world and in the world to come." If by "life" be meant this earthly life, it is evident that death must needs overtake it.[60]

This Passing Life

Say: Rejoice not in the things ye possess; tonight they are yours, tomorrow others will possess them. Thus warneth you He Who is the All-Knowing, the All-Informed. Say: Can ye claim that what ye own is lasting or secure? Nay! By Myself, the All-Merciful. The days of your life flee away as a breath of wind, and all your pomp and glory shall be folded up as were the pomp and glory of those gone before you. Reflect, O people! What hath become of your bygone days, your lost centuries? Happy the days that have been consecrated to the remembrance of God, and blessed the hours which have been spent in praise of Him Who is the All-Wise. By My life! Neither the pomp of the mighty, nor the wealth of the rich, nor even the ascendancy of the ungodly will endure. All will perish, at a word from Him. He, verily, is the All-Powerful, the All-Compelling, the Almighty. What advantage is there in the earthly things which men possess? That which shall profit them, they have utterly neglected. Erelong, they will awake from their slumber, and find themselves unable to obtain that which hath escaped them in the days of their Lord, the Almighty, the All-Praised. Did they but know it, they would renounce their all, that their names may be mentioned before His throne. They, verily, are accounted among the dead.[61]

Deeds That Endure

Live ye one with another, O people, in radiance and joy. By My life! All that are on earth shall pass away, while good deeds alone shall endure; to the truth of My words God doth Himself bear witness.[62]

The Day of Meritorious Deeds

Say: This is the Day of meritorious deeds, did ye but know it. This is the Day of the glorification of God and of the exposition of His Word, could ye but perceive it. Abandon the things current amongst men and hold fast unto that which God, the Help in Peril, the Self-Subsisting, hath enjoined upon you. The day is fast approaching when all the treasures of the earth shall be of no profit to you. Unto this beareth witness the Lord of Names, He Who proclaimeth: Verily, no God is there besides Him, the Sovereign Truth, the Knower of things unseen.[63]

The Return to Dust

Walk ye, during the few remaining days of your life, in the ways of the one true God. Your days shall pass away as have the days of them who were before you. To dust shall ye return, even as your fathers of old did return.[64]

* * *

Wish not for others what ye wish not for yourselves; fear God, and be not of the prideful. Ye are all created out of water, and unto dust shall ye return. Reflect upon the end that awaiteth you, and walk not in the ways of the oppressor.[65]

Bring Forth Immortal Fruits

Say, I swear by the righteousness of God! Ere long the pomp of the ministers of state and the ascendancy of the rulers shall pass away, the palaces of the potentates shall be laid waste and the imposing buildings of the emperors reduced to dust, but what shall endure is that which We have ordained for you in the Kingdom. It behoveth you, O people, to make the utmost endeavor that your names may be mentioned before the Throne and ye may bring forth that which will immortalize your memories throughout the eternity of God, the Lord of all being.[66]

Blessings For Pure Actions

We verily behold your actions. If We perceive from them the sweet smelling savor of purity and holiness, We will most certainly bless you. Then will the tongues of the inmates of Paradise utter your praise and magnify your names amidst them who have drawn nigh unto God.[67]

It Shall be Known to You

He, verily, hath willed for you that which is yet beyond your knowledge, but which shall be known to you when, after this fleeting life, your souls soar heavenwards and the trappings of your earthly joys are folded up. Thus admonisheth you He in Whose possession is the Guarded Tablet.[68]

The Return to God

"Verily, we are God's," and abide within the exalted habitation: "And unto Him we do return."[69]

* * *

All things proceed from God and unto Him they return. He is the source of all things and in Him all things are ended.[70]

The Cup of Everlasting Life

The hands of bounty have borne round the cup of everlasting life. Approach, and quaff your fill. Drink with healthy relish, O ye that are the very incarnations of longing, ye who are the embodiments of vehement desire![71]

The Fountain of Everlasting Life

He is indeed as one dead who, at the wondrous dawn of this Revelation, hath failed to be quickened by its soul-stirring breeze. He is indeed a captive who hath not recognized the Supreme Redeemer, but hath suffered his soul to be bound, distressed and helpless, in the fetters of his desires.

O My servants! Whoso hath tasted of this Fountain hath attained unto everlasting Life, and whoso hath refused to drink therefrom is even as the dead. Say: O ye workers of iniquity! Covetousness hath hindered you from giving a hearing ear unto the sweet voice of Him Who is the All-Sufficing. Wash it away from your hearts, that His Divine secret may be made known unto you. Behold Him manifest and resplendent as the sun in all its glory.[72]

Part II

Selections From the
Writings of the Báb

Devoid of Life

Say, the power of God is in the hearts of those who believe in the unity of God and bear witness that no God is there but Him, while the hearts of them that associate partners with God are impotent, devoid of life on this earth, for assuredly they are dead.[1]

The Exalted Paradise
And the Fierce Fire

There is no paradise, in the estimation of the believers in the Divine Unity, more exalted than to obey God's commandments, and there is no fire in the eyes of those who have known God and His signs, fiercer than to transgress His laws and to oppress another soul, even to the extent of a mustard seed. On the Day of Resurrection God will, in truth, judge all men, and we all verily plead for His grace.[2]

* * *

In this Day therefore I bear witness unto My creatures, for the witness of no one other than Myself hath been or shall ever be worthy of mention in My presence. I affirm that no Paradise is more sublime for My creatures than to stand before My face and to believe in My holy Words, while no fire hath been or will be fiercer for them than to be veiled from the Manifestation of My exalted Self and to disbelieve in My Words.[3]

The Wondrous Paradise

There is no paradise more wondrous for any soul than to be exposed to God's Manifestation in His Day, to hear His verses and believe in them, to attain His presence, which is naught but the presence of God, to sail upon the sea of the heavenly kingdom of His good-pleasure, and to partake of the choice fruits of the paradise of His divine Oneness.[4]

Attaining Paradise

No created thing shall ever attain its paradise unless it appeareth in its highest prescribed degree of perfection. For instance, this crystal representeth the paradise of the stone whereof its substance is composed. Likewise there are various stages in the paradise for the crystal itself...So long as it was stone it was worthless, but if it attaineth the excellence of ruby—a potentiality which is latent in it—how much a carat will it be worth? Consider likewise every created thing.

Man's highest station, however, is attained through faith in God in every Dispensation and by acceptance of what hath been revealed by Him, and not through learning; inasmuch as in every nation there are learned men who are versed in divers sciences. Nor is it attainable through wealth; for it is similarly evident that among the various classes in every nation there are those possessed of riches. Likewise are other transitory things.

True knowledge, therefore, is the knowledge of God, and this is none other than the recognition of His Manifestation in each Dispensation. Nor is there any wealth save in poverty in all save God and sanctity from aught else but Him—a state that can be realized only when demonstrated towards Him Who is the Dayspring of His Revelation.[5]

Resurrection, Hell-Fire, And Paradise

True resurrection from the sepulchers means to be quickened in conformity with His Will, through the power of His utterance.

Paradise is attainment of His good-pleasure and everlasting hell-fire His judgment through justice.

The Day He revealeth Himself is Resurrection Day which shall last as long as He ordaineth.

Everything belongeth unto Him and is fashioned by Him. All besides Him are His creatures.[6]

The Day of Resurrection

The Day of Resurrection is a day on which the sun riseth and setteth like unto any other day. How oft hath the Day of Resurrection dawned, and the people of the land where it occurred did not learn of the event. Had they heard, they would not have believed, and thus they were not told![7]

* * *

...what is meant by the Day of Resurrection is this, that from the time of the appearance of Him Who is the Tree of divine Reality, at whatever period and under whatever name, until the moment of His disappearance, is the Day of Resurrection.

For example, from the inception of the mission of Jesus—may peace be upon Him—till the day of His ascension was the Resurrection of Moses. For during that period the Revelation of God shone forth through the appearance of that divine Reality, Who rewarded by His Word everyone who believed in Moses, and punished by His Word everyone who did not believe; inasmuch as God's Testimony for that Day was that which He had solemnly affirmed in the Gospel. And from the inception of the Revelation of the Apostle of God—may the blessings of God be upon Him—till the day of His ascension was the Resurrection of Jesus—peace be upon Him—wherein the Tree of divine Reality appeared in the person of Muhammad, rewarding by His Word everyone who was a believer in Jesus, and punishing by His Word everyone who was not a believer in Him.[8]

Respect for the Body

As this physical frame is the throne of the inner temple, whatever occurs to the former is felt by the latter. In reality that which takes delight in joy or is saddened by pain is the inner temple of the body, not the body itself. Since this physical body is the throne whereon the inner temple is established, God hath ordained that the body be preserved to the extent possible, so that nothing that causeth repugnance may be experienced. The inner temple beholdeth its physical frame, which is its throne. Thus, if the latter is accorded respect, it is as if the former is the recipient. The converse is likewise true.

Therefore, it hath been ordained that the dead body should be treated with the utmost honor and respect.[9]

Every Deed Rewarded

Say, this earthly life shall come to an end, and everyone shall expire and return unto my Lord God Who will reward with the choicest gifts the deeds of those who endure with patience. Verily thy God assigneth the measure of all created things as He willeth, by virtue of His behest; and those who conform to the good-pleasure of your Lord, they are indeed among the blissful.[10]

Every Act Preserved

O peoples of the world! Whatsoever ye have offered up in the way of the One True God, ye shall indeed find preserved by God, the Preserver, intact at God's Holy Gate.[11]

Unto Him Shall All Return

Say, God is the Lord and all are worshippers unto Him.

Say, God is the True One and all pay homage unto Him.

This is God, your Lord, and unto Him shall ye return.

Is there any doubt concerning God? He hath created you and all things. The Lord of all worlds is He.[12]

* * *

All men have proceeded from God and unto Him shall all return. All shall appear before Him for judgment. He is the Lord of the Day of Resurrection, of Regeneration and of Reckoning, and His revealed Word is the Balance.[13]

In the Presence of God

This mortal life is sure to perish; its pleasures are bound to fade away and ere long ye shall return unto God, distressed with pangs of remorse, for presently ye shall be roused from your slumber, and ye shall soon find yourselves in the presence of God and will be asked of your doings.[14]

Entering Paradise

Verily, on the First Day We flung open the gates of Paradise unto all the peoples of the world, and exclaimed: 'O all ye created things! Strive to gain admittance into Paradise, since ye have, during all your lives, held fast unto virtuous deeds in order to attain unto it.' Surely all men yearn to enter therein, but alas, they are unable to do so by reason of that which their hands have wrought. Shouldst thou, however, gain a true understanding of God in thine heart of hearts, ere He hath manifested Himself, thou wouldst be able to recognize Him, visible and resplendent, when He unveileth Himself before the eyes of all men.[15]

Inmates of the All-Highest Paradise

Whenever the faithful hear the verses of this Book being recited, their eyes will overflow with tears and their hearts will be deeply touched by Him Who is the Most Great Remembrance for the love they cherish for God, the All-Praised. He is God, the All-Knowing, the Eternal. They are indeed the inmates of the all-highest Paradise wherein they will abide for ever. Verily they will see naught therein save that which hath proceeded from God, nothing that will lie beyond the compass of their understanding. There they will meet the believers in Paradise, who will address them with the words 'Peace, Peace' lingering on their lips...[16]

Belief Rewarded

...Verily God shall soon reward thee and those who have believed in His signs with an excellent reward from His presence. Assuredly no God is there other than Him, the All-Possessing, the Most Generous. The revelations of His bounty pervade all created things; He is the Merciful, the Compassionate.[17]

Everlasting Reunion With God

Deliver the summons of the most exalted Word unto the handmaids among Thy kindred, caution them against the Most Great Fire and announce unto them the joyful tidings that following this mighty Covenant there shall be everlasting reunion with God in the Paradise of His good-pleasure, nigh unto the Seat of Holiness. Verily God, the Lord of creation, is potent over all things.[18]

The Life to Come More Advantageous

The life to come is indeed far more advantageous unto Thee and unto such as follow Thy Cause than this earthly life and its pleasures. This is what hath been foreordained according to the dispensations of Providence...[19]

Inscrutable Gardens

O My servants! Seek ye earnestly this highest reward, as I have indeed created for the Remembrance of God gardens which remain inscrutable to anyone save Myself, and naught therein hath been made lawful unto anyone except those whose lives have been sacrificed in His Path. Hence beseech ye God, the Most Exalted, that He may grant you this meritorious reward, and He is in truth the Most High, the Most Great.[20]

True Death

True death is realized when a person dieth to himself at the time of His Revelation in such wise that he seeketh naught except Him.[21]*

---

*This station is the dying from self and the living in God, the being poor in self and rich in the Desired One.[22]   Bahá'u'lláh

Part III

Selections From Written And Spoken Words of ‘Abdu’l-Bahá

Man, a Spiritual Being

Man—the true man—is soul, not body; though physically man belongs to the animal kingdom, yet his soul lifts him above the rest of creation. Behold how the light of the sun illuminates the world of matter: even so doth the Divine Light shed its rays in the kingdom of the soul. The soul it is which makes the human creature a celestial entity!

By the power of the Holy Spirit, working through his soul, man is able to perceive the Divine reality of things. All great works of art and science are witnesses to this power of the Spirit. The same Spirit gives Eternal Life.[1]

Nearest to the Nature of God

The superiority of man over the rest of the created world is seen again in this, that man has a soul in which dwells the divine spirit; the souls of the lower creatures are inferior in their essence.

There is no doubt then, that of all created beings man is the nearest to the nature of God, and therefore receives a greater gift of the Divine Bounty.

The mineral kingdom possesses the power of existing. The plant has the power of existing and growing. The animal, in addition to existence and growth, has the capacity of moving about, and the use of the faculties of the senses. In the human kingdom we find all the attributes of the lower worlds, with much more added thereto. Man is the sum of every previous creation, for he contains them all.

To man is given the special gift of the intellect by which he is able to receive a larger share of the light Divine. The Perfect Man is as a polished mirror reflecting the Sun of Truth, manifesting the attributes of God.[2]

The Reality of Man

The reality of man is his thought, not his material body. The thought force and the animal force are partners. Although man is part of the animal creation, he possesses a power of thought superior to all other created beings.[3]

The Potential of a Pure Soul

Souls are like unto mirrors, and the bounty of God is like unto the sun. When the mirrors pass beyond all coloring and attain purity and polish, and are confronted with the sun, they will reflect in full perfection its light and glory. In this condition one should not consider the mirror, but the power of the light of the sun, which hath penetrated the mirror, making it a reflector of the heavenly glory.[4]

Man, the Perfect Mirror of Divine Attributes

We have many times demonstrated and established that man is the noblest of beings, the sum of all perfections, and that all beings and all existences are the centers from which the glory of God is reflected—that is to say, the signs of the Divinity of God are apparent in the realities of things and of creatures. Just as the terrestrial globe is the place where the rays of the sun are reflected—as its light, its heat and its influence are apparent and visible in all the atoms of the earth—so, in the same way, the atoms of beings, in this infinite space, proclaim and prove one of the divine perfections. Nothing is deprived of this benefit; either it is a sign of the mercy of God, or it is a sign of His power, His greatness, His justice, His nurturing providence; or it is a sign of the generosity of God, His vision, His hearing, His knowledge, His grace and so on.

Without doubt each being is the center of the shining forth of the glory of God—that is to say, the perfections of God appear from it and are resplendent in it. It is like the sun, which is resplendent in the desert, upon the sea, in the trees, in the fruits and blossoms, and in all earthly things. The world, indeed each existing being, proclaims to us one of the names of God, but the reality of man is the collective reality, the general reality, and is the center where the glory of all the perfections of God shine forth—that is to say, for each name, each attribute, each perfection which we affirm of God there exists a sign in man. If it were otherwise, man could not imagine these perfections and could not understand them. So we say that God is the seer, and the eye is the sign of His vision; if this sight were not in man, how could we imagine the vision of God? For the blind (that is, one born blind) cannot imagine sight; and the deaf (that is, one deaf from birth) cannot imagine hearing; and the dead cannot realize life. Consequently, the Divinity of God, which is the sum of all perfections, reflects itself in the reality of man—that is to say, the Essence of Oneness is the gathering of all perfections, and from this unity He casts a reflection upon the human reality. Man, then, is the perfect mirror facing the Sun of Truth and is the center of radiation: the Sun of Truth shines in this mirror. The reflection of the divine perfections appears in the reality of man, so he is the representative of God, the messenger of God. If man did not exist, the universe would be without result, for the object of existence is the appearance of the perfections of God.[5]

Man, the End of Imperfection And the Beginning of Perfection

When we consider beings with the seeing eye, we observe that they are limited to three sorts—that is to say, as a whole they are either mineral, vegetable or animal, each of these three classes containing species. Man is the highest species because he is the possessor of the perfections of all the classes—that is, he has a body which grows and which feels. As well as having the perfections of the mineral, of the vegetable and of the animal, he also possesses an especial excellence which the other beings are without—that is, the intellectual perfections. Therefore, man is the most noble of beings.

Man is in the highest degree of materiality, and at the beginning of spirituality—that is to say, he is the end of imperfection and the beginning of perfection. He is at the last degree of darkness, and at the beginning of light; that is why it has been said that the condition of man is the end of the night and the beginning of day, meaning that he is the sum of all the degrees of imperfection, and that he possesses the degrees of perfection. He has the animal side as well as the angelic side, and the aim of an educator is to so train human souls that their angelic aspect may overcome their animal side. Then if the divine power in man, which is his essential perfection, overcomes the satanic power, which is absolute imperfection, he becomes the most excellent among the creatures; but if the satanic power overcomes the divine power, he becomes the lowest of the creatures. That is why he is the end of imperfection and the beginning of perfection. Not in any other of the species in the world of existence is there such a difference, contrast, contradiction and opposition as in the species of man. Thus the reflection of the Divine Light was in man, as in Christ, and see how loved and honored He is! At the same time we see man worshipping a stone, a clod of earth or a tree. How vile he is, in that his object of worship should be the lowest existence—that is, a stone or clay, without spirit; a mountain, a forest or a tree. What shame is greater for man than to worship the lowest existences? In the same way, knowledge is a quality of man, and so is ignorance; truthfulness is a quality of man; so is falsehood; trustworthiness and treachery, justice and injustice, are qualities of man, and so forth. Briefly, all the perfections and virtues, and all the vices, are qualities of man.

Consider equally the differences between individual men. Christ was in the form of man, and Caiaphas was in the form of man; Moses and Pharaoh, Abel and Cain, Bahá'u'lláh and Yahyá,* were men.

Man is said to be the greatest representative of God, and he is the Book of Creation because all the mysteries of beings exist in him. If he comes under the shadow of the True Educator and is rightly trained, he becomes the essence of essences, the light of lights, the spirit of spirits; he becomes the center of the divine appearances, the source of spiritual qualities, the rising-place of heavenly lights, and the receptacle of divine inspirations. If he is deprived of this education, he becomes the manifestation of satanic qualities, the sum of animal vices, and the source of all dark conditions.

The reason of the mission of the Prophets is to educate men, so that this piece of coal may become a diamond, and this fruitless tree may be engrafted and yield the sweetest, most delicious fruits. When man reaches the noblest state in the world of humanity, then he can make further progress in the conditions of perfection, but not in state; for such states are limited, but the divine perfections are endless.

Both before and after putting off this material form, there is progress in perfection but not in state. So beings are consummated in perfect man. There is no other being higher than a perfect man. But man when he has reached this state can still make progress in perfections but not in state because there is no state higher than that of a perfect man to which he can transfer himself. He only progresses in the state of humanity, for the human perfections are infinite. Thus, however learned a man may be, we can imagine one more learned.

Hence, as the perfections of humanity are endless, man can also make progress in perfections after leaving this world.[6]

---

*Mírzá Yahyá (Subh-i-Azal), Bahá'u'lláh's half-brother and His bitter enemy.

All Things Are in Motion

Know that nothing which exists remains in a state of repose—
that is to say, all things are in motion. Everything is either
growing or declining; all things are either coming from nonexistence into being, or going from existence into nonexistence.
So this flower, this hyacinth, during a certain period of time
was coming from the world of nonexistence into being, and
now it is going from being into nonexistence. This state of
motion is said to be essential—that is, natural; it cannot be
separated from beings because it is their essential requirement,
as it is the essential requirement of fire to burn.

Thus it is established that this movement is necessary to
existence, which is either growing or declining. Now, as the
spirit continues to exist after death, it necessarily progresses
or declines; and in the other world to cease to progress is
the same as to decline; but it never leaves its own condition,
in which it continues to develop. For example, the reality of
the spirit of Peter, however far it may progress, will not
reach to the condition of the Reality of Christ; it progresses
only in its own environment.

Look at this mineral. However far it may evolve, it only
evolves in its own condition; you cannot bring the crystal to
a state where it can attain to sight. This is impossible. So the
moon which is in the heavens, however far it might evolve,
could never become a luminous sun, but in its own condition
it has apogee and perigee. However far the disciples might
progress, they could never become Christ. It is true that
coal could become a diamond, but both are in the mineral
condition, and their component elements are the same.[7]

Evolution of the Soul

As to the soul of man after death, it remains in the degree
of purity to which it has evolved during life in the physical
body, and after it is freed from the body it remains plunged
in the ocean of God's Mercy.

From the moment the soul leaves the body and arrives in the Heavenly World, its evolution is spiritual, and that evolution is: *The approaching unto God.*

In the physical creation, evolution is from one degree of perfection to another. The mineral passes with its mineral perfections to the vegetable; the vegetable, with its perfections, passes to the animal world, and so on to that of humanity. This world is full of seeming contradictions; in each of these kingdoms (mineral, vegetable and animal) life exists in its degree; though when compared to the life in a man, the earth appears to be dead, yet she, too, lives and has a life of her own. In this world things live and die, and live again in other forms of life, but in the world of the spirit it is quite otherwise.

The soul does not evolve from degree to degree as a law—it only evolves nearer to God, by the Mercy and Bounty of God.

It is my earnest prayer that we may all be in the Kingdom of God, and near Him.[8]

* * *

But regarding the progress of the spirit in the world of the Kingdom after its ascension...It is like unto the progress of the child from the world of the fetus to the world of maturity and intelligence, from the world of ignorance to the world of knowledge, from the station of imperfection to the pinnacle of perfection.

As Divine Perfections are infinite, therefore the progress of the spirit is *limitless.*[9]

Evolution of the Spirit

Tonight I will speak of the evolution or progress of the spirit.

Absolute repose does not exist in nature. All things either make progress or lose ground. Everything moves forward or backward, nothing is without motion. From his birth, a man progresses physically until he reaches maturity, then, having arrived at the prime of his life, he begins to decline, the strength and powers of his body decrease, and he gradually arrives at the hour of death. Likewise a plant progresses from the seed to maturity, then its life begins to lessen until it fades and dies. A bird soars to a certain height and having reached the highest possible point in its flight, begins its descent to earth.

Thus it is evident that movement is essential to all existence. All material things progress to a certain point, then begin to decline. This is the law which governs the whole physical creation.

Now let us consider the soul. We have seen that movement is essential to existence; nothing that has life is without motion. All creation, whether of the mineral, vegetable or animal kingdom, is compelled to obey the law of motion; it must either ascend or descend. But with the human soul, there is no decline. Its only movement is towards perfection; growth and progress alone constitute the motion of the soul.

Divine perfection is infinite, therefore the progress of the soul is also infinite. From the very birth of a human being the soul progresses, the intellect grows and knowledge increases. When the body dies the soul lives on. All the differing degrees of created physical beings are limited, but the soul is limitless!

In the world of spirit there is no retrogression. The world of mortality is a world of contradictions, of opposites; motion being compulsory everything must either go forward or retreat. In the realm of spirit there is no retreat possible, all movement is bound to be towards a perfect state. 'Progress' is the expression of spirit in the world of matter. The intelligence of man, his reasoning powers, his knowledge, his scientific achievements, all these being manifestations of the spirit, partake of the inevitable law of spiritual progress and are, therefore, of necessity, immortal...

My hope for you is that you will progress in the world of spirit, as well as in the world of matter; that your intelligence will develop, your knowledge will augment, and your understanding be widened.[10]

Praying for Parents

...a father and mother endure the greatest troubles and hardships for their children; and often when the children have reached the age of maturity, the parents pass on to the other world. Rarely does it happen that a father and mother in this world see the reward of the care and trouble they have undergone for their children. Therefore, children, in return for this care and trouble, must show forth charity and beneficence, and must implore pardon and forgiveness for their parents. So you ought, in return for the love and kindness shown you by your father, to give to the poor for his sake, with greatest submission and humility implore pardon and remission of sins, and ask for the supreme mercy.[11]

Means of Progress
in the Next Kingdom

The wealth of the other world is nearness to God. Consequently, it is certain that those who are near the Divine Court are allowed to intercede, and this intercession is approved by God. But intercession in the other world is not like intercession in this world. It is another thing, another reality, which cannot be expressed in words.

If a wealthy man at the time of his death bequeaths a gift to the poor and miserable, and gives a part of his wealth to be spent for them, perhaps this action may be the cause of his pardon and forgiveness, and of his progress in the Divine Kingdom...

It is even possible that the condition of those who have died in sin and unbelief may become changed—that is to say, they may become the object of pardon through the bounty of God, not through His justice—for bounty is giving without desert, and justice is giving what is deserved. As we have power to pray for these souls here, so likewise we shall possess the same power in the other world, which is the Kingdom of God. Are not all the people in that world the creatures of God? Therefore, in that world also they can make progress. As here they can receive light by their supplications, there also they can plead for forgiveness and receive light through entreaties and supplications. Thus as souls in this world, through the help of the supplications, the entreaties and the prayers of the holy ones, can acquire development, so is it the same after death. Through their own prayers and supplications they can also progress, more especially when they are the object of the intercession of the Holy Manifestations.[12]

* * *

Question: Through what means will the spirit of man—that is to say, the rational soul—after departing from this mortal world, make progress?

Answer: The progress of man's spirit in the divine world, after the severance of its connection with the body of dust, is through the bounty and grace of the Lord alone, or through the intercession and the sincere prayers of other human souls, or through the charities and important good works which are performed in its name.[13]

The Endless Perfections

Know that the conditions of existence are limited to the conditions of servitude, of prophethood and of Deity, but the divine and the contingent perfections are unlimited. When you reflect deeply, you discover that also outwardly the perfections of existence are also unlimited, for you cannot find a being so perfect that you cannot imagine a superior one. For example, you cannot see a ruby in the mineral kingdom, a rose in the vegetable kingdom, or a nightingale in the animal kingdom, without imagining that there might be better specimens. As the divine bounties are endless, so human perfections are endless. If it were possible to reach a limit of perfection, then one of the realities of the beings might reach the condition of being independent of God, and the contingent might attain to the condition of the absolute. But for every being there is a point which it cannot overpass—that is to say, he who is in the condition of servitude, however far he may progress in gaining limitless perfections, will never reach the condition of Deity. It is the same with the other beings. A mineral, however far it may progress in the mineral kingdom, cannot gain the vegetable power. Also in a flower, however far it may progress in the vegetable kingdom, no power of the senses will appear. So this silver mineral cannot gain hearing or sight; it can only improve in its own condition and become a perfect mineral, but it cannot acquire the power of growth, or the power of sensation, or attain to life; it can only progress in its own condition.

For example, Peter cannot become Christ. All that he can do is, in the condition of servitude, to attain endless perfections; for every existing reality is capable of making progress. As the spirit of man after putting off this material form has an everlasting life, certainly any existing being is capable of making progress; therefore, it is permitted to ask for advancement, forgiveness, mercy, beneficence and blessings for a man after his death because existence is capable of progression. That is why in the prayers of Bahá'u'lláh forgiveness and remission of sins are asked for those who have died.[14]

Progress Through Suffering

'Does the soul progress more through sorrow or through the joy in this world?'

'Abdu'l-Bahá: 'The mind and spirit of man advance when he is tried by suffering. The more the ground is ploughed the better the seed will grow, the better the harvest will be. Just as the plough furrows the earth deeply, purifying it of weeds and thistles, so suffering and tribulation free man

from the petty affairs of this worldly life until he arrives at a state of complete detachment. His attitude in this world will be that of divine happiness. Man is, so to speak, unripe: the heat of the fire of suffering will mature him. Look back to the times past and you will find that the greatest men have suffered most.'[15]

The Two Wings of the Soul

Regarding the "two wings" of the soul: These signify wings of ascent. One is the wing of knowledge, the other of faith, as this is the means of the ascent of the human soul to the lofty station of divine perfections.[16]

Everlasting Life

As to thy question, doth every soul without exception achieve life everlasting? Know thou that immortality belongeth to those souls in whom hath been breathed the spirit of life from God. All save these are lifeless—they are the dead, even as Christ hath explained in the Gospel text. He whose eyes the Lord hath opened will see the souls of men in the stations they will occupy after their release from the body. He will find the living ones thriving within the precincts of their Lord, and the dead sunk down in the lowest abyss of perdition.[17]

* * *

Undoubtedly, those souls who are under the shadow of the Blessed Cause, believing and assured, firm and steadfast, and living in accord with the Divine exhortations and advices, all of them are confirmed in the Everlasting Life.[18]

Man's Supreme Station

A man should pause and reflect and be just: his Lord, out of measureless grace, has made him a human being and honored him with the words: "Verily, We created man in the goodliest of forms"—and caused His mercy which rises out of the dawn of oneness to shine down upon him, until he became the wellspring of the words of God and the place where the mysteries of heaven alighted, and on the morning of creation he was covered with the rays of the qualities of perfection and the graces of holiness.[19]

The Kingdom of Heaven

O thou who seekest the Kingdom of heaven! This world is even as the body of man, and the Kingdom of God is as the spirit of life. See how dark and narrow is the physical world of man's body, and what a prey it is to diseases and ills. On the other hand, how fresh and bright is the realm of the human spirit. Judge thou from this metaphor how the world of the Kingdom hath shone down, and how its laws have been made to work in this nether realm. Although the spirit is hidden from view, still its commandments shine out like rays of light upon the world of the human body. In the same way, although the Kingdom of heaven is hidden from the sight of this unwitting people, still, to him who seeth with the inner eye, it is plain as day.

Wherefore dwell thou ever in the Kingdom, and be thou oblivious of this world below. Be thou so wholly absorbed in the emanations of the spirit that nothing in the world of man will distract thee.[20]

Man Always in Need of God

Moreover, as people in this world are in need of God, they will also need Him in the other world. The creatures are always in need, and God is absolutely independent, whether in this world or in the world to come.[21]

Knowledge of God
Accessible to the Pure

Likewise, ask thou of God that the magnet of His love should draw unto thee the knowledge of Him. Once a soul becometh holy in all things, purified, sanctified, the gates of the knowledge of God will open wide before his eyes.[22]

Riches A Barrier to the Kingdom

Bahá'u'lláh hath been made manifest to all mankind and He hath invited all to the table of God, the banquet of Divine bounty. Today, however, most of those who sit at that table are the poor, and this is why Christ hath said blessed are the poor, for riches do prevent the rich from entering the Kingdom; and again, He saith, 'It is easier for a camel to go through the eye of a needle, than for a rich man to enter into the Kingdom of God.'* If, however, the wealth of this world, and worldly glory and repute, do not block his entry therein, that rich man will be favored at the Holy Threshold and accepted by the Lord of the Kingdom.[23]

---

*Matthew 19:24; Mark 10:25.

Each Soul to Stand Alone Before God

Therefore, it follows that as each soul has its own possibility of development, it is necessary for each soul to stand alone before God. No one can stand for you in the Presence of God in the 'Last Day.'[24]

Eternal Life and Entrance Into the Kingdom of God

You question about eternal life and the entrance into the Kingdom. The outer expression used for the Kingdom is heaven; but this is a comparison and similitude, not a reality or fact, for the Kingdom is not a material place; it is sanctified from time and place. It is a spiritual world, a divine world, and the center of the Sovereignty of God; it is freed from body and that which is corporeal, and it is purified and sanctified from the imaginations of the human world. To be limited to place is a property of bodies and not of spirits. Place and time surround the body, not the mind and spirit. Observe that the body of man is confined to a small place; it covers only two spans of earth. But the spirit and mind of man travel to all countries and regions—even through the limitless space of the heavens—surround all that exists, and make discoveries in the exalted spheres and infinite distances. This is because the spirit has no place; it is placeless; and for the spirit the earth and the heaven are as one since it makes discoveries in both. But the body is limited to a place and does not know that which is beyond it.

For life is of two kinds: that of the body and that of the spirit. The life of the body is material life, but the life of the spirit expresses the existence of the Kingdom, which consists in receiving the Spirit of God and becoming vivified by the breath of the Holy Spirit. Although the material life has existence, it is pure nonexistence and absolute death for the holy saints. So man exists, and this stone also exists, but what a difference between the existence of man and that of the stone! Though the stone exists, in relation to the existence of man it is nonexistent.

The meaning of eternal life is the gift of the Holy Spirit, as the flower receives the gift of the season, the air, and the breezes of spring. Consider: this flower had life in the beginning like the life of the mineral; but by the coming of the season of spring, of the bounty of the clouds of the springtime, and of the heat of the glowing sun, it attained to another life of the utmost freshness, delicacy and fragrance. The first life of the flower, in comparison to the second life, is death.

The meaning is that the life of the Kingdom is the life of the spirit, the eternal life, and that it is purified from place, like the spirit of man which has no place. For if you examine the human body, you will not find a special spot or locality for the spirit, for it has never had a place; it is immaterial. It has a connection with the body like that of the sun with this mirror. The sun is not within the mirror, but it has a connection with the mirror.

In the same way the world of the Kingdom is sanctified from everything that can be perceived by the eye or by the other senses—hearing, smell, taste or touch. The mind which is in man, the existence of which is recognized— where is it in him? If you examine the body with the eye, the ear or the other senses, you will not find it; nevertheless, it exists. Therefore, the mind has no place, but it is connected with the brain. The Kingdom is also like this. In the same way love has no place, but it is connected with the heart; so the Kingdom has no place, but is connected with man.

Entrance into the Kingdom is through the love of God, through detachment, through holiness and chastity, through truthfulness, purity, steadfastness, faithfulness and the sacrifice of life.

These explanations show that man is immortal and lives eternally. For those who believe in God, who have love of God, and faith, life is excellent—that is, it is eternal; but to those souls who are veiled from God, although they have life, it is dark, and in comparison with the life of believers it is nonexistence.

For example, the eye and the nail are living; but the life of the nail in relation to the life of the eye is nonexistent. This stone and this man both exist; but the stone in relation to the existence of man is nonexistent; it has no being; for when man dies, and his body is destroyed and annihilated, it becomes like stone and earth. Therefore, it is clear that although the mineral exists, in relation to man it is nonexistent.

In the same way, the souls who are veiled from God, although they exist in this world and in the world after death, are, in comparison with the holy existence of the children of the Kingdom of God, nonexisting and separated from God.[25]

Attributes Needed in the Kingdom of Heaven

In the world of existence man has traversed successive degrees until he has attained the human kingdom. In each degree of his progression he has developed capacity for advancement to the next station and condition. While in the kingdom of the mineral he was attaining the capacity for promotion into the degree of the vegetable. In the kingdom of the vegetable he underwent preparation for the world of the animal, and from thence he has come onward to the human degree, or kingdom. Throughout this journey of progression he has ever and always been potentially man.

In the beginning of his human life man was embryonic in the world of the matrix. There he received capacity and endowment for the reality of human existence. The forces and powers necessary for this world were bestowed upon him in that limited condition. In this world he needed eyes; he received them potentially in the other. He needed ears; he obtained them there in readiness and preparation for his new existence. The powers requisite in this world were conferred upon him in the world of the matrix so that when he entered this realm of real existence he not only possessed all necessary functions and powers but found provision for his material sustenance awaiting him.

Therefore, in this world he must prepare himself for the life beyond. That which he needs in the world of the Kingdom must be obtained here. Just as he prepared himself in the world of the matrix by acquiring forces necessary in this sphere of existence, so, likewise, the indispensable forces of the divine existence must be potentially attained in this world.

What is he in need of in the Kingdom which transcends the life and limitation of this mortal sphere? That world beyond is a world of sanctity and radiance; therefore, it is necessary that in this world he should acquire these divine attributes. In that world there is need of spirituality, faith, assurance, the knowledge and love of God. These he must attain in this world so that after his ascension from the earthly to the heavenly Kingdom he shall find all that is needful in that eternal life ready for him.

That divine world is manifestly a world of lights; therefore, man has need of illumination here. That is a world of love; the love of God is essential. It is a world of perfections; virtues, or perfections, must be acquired. That world is vivified by the breaths of the Holy Spirit; in this world we must seek them. That is the Kingdom of everlasting life; it must be attained during this vanishing existence.

By what means can man acquire these things? How shall he obtain these merciful gifts and powers? First, through the knowledge of God. Second, through the love of God. Third, through faith. Fourth, through philanthropic deeds. Fifth, through self-sacrifice. Sixth, through severance from this world. Seventh, through sanctity and holiness. Unless he acquires these forces and attains to these requirements, he will surely be deprived of the life that is eternal. But if he possesses the knowledge of God, becomes ignited through the fire of the love of God, witnesses the great and mighty signs of the Kingdom, becomes the cause of love among mankind and lives in the utmost state of sanctity and holiness, he shall surely attain to second birth, be baptized by the Holy Spirit and enjoy everlasting existence.

Is it not astonishing that although man has been created for the knowledge and love of God, for the virtues of the human world, for spirituality, heavenly illumination and eternal life, nevertheless, he continues ignorant and negligent of all this? Consider how he seeks knowledge of everything except knowledge of God. For instance, his utmost desire is to penetrate the mysteries of the lowest strata of the earth. Day by day he strives to know what can be found ten meters below the surface, what he can discover within the stone, what he can learn by archaeological research in the dust. He puts forth arduous labors to fathom terrestrial mysteries but is not at all concerned about knowing the mysteries of the Kingdom, traversing the illimitable fields of the eternal world, becoming informed of the divine realities, discovering the secrets of God, attaining the knowledge of God, witnessing the splendors of the Sun of Truth and realizing the glories of everlasting life. He is unmindful and thoughtless of these. How much he is attracted to the mysteries of matter, and how completely unaware he is of the mysteries of Divinity! Nay, he is utterly negligent and oblivious of the secrets of Divinity. How great his ignorance! How conducive to his degradation! It is as if a kind and loving father had provided a library of wonderful books for his son in order that he might be informed of the mysteries of creation, at the same time surrounding him with every means of comfort and enjoyment, but the son amuses himself with pebbles and playthings, neglectful of all his father's gifts and provision. How ignorant and heedless is man! The Father has willed for him eternal glory, and he is content with blindness and deprivation. The Father has built for him a royal palace, but he is playing with the dust; prepared for him garments of silk, but he prefers to remain unclothed; provided for him delicious foods and fruits, while he seeks sustenance in the grasses of the field.[26]

Acquainted With All Mysteries

The mysteries of which man is heedless in the earthly world, those will he discover in the heavenly world, and there will he be informed of the secrets of the truth; how much more will he recognize or discover persons with whom he has been associated. Undoubtedly the holy souls who find a pure eye and are favored with insight will, in the kingdom of lights, be acquainted with all mysteries, and will seek the bounty of witnessing the reality of every great soul. They will even manifestly behold the Beauty of God in that world. Likewise will they find all the friends of God, both those of the former and recent times, present in the heavenly assemblage.

The difference and distinction between men will naturally become realized after their departure from this mortal world. But this distinction is not in respect to place, but in respect to the soul and conscience. For the Kingdom of God is sanctified (or free) from time and place; it is another world and another universe. And know thou for a certainty that in the divine worlds the spiritual beloved ones will recognize one another, and will seek union with each other, but a spiritual union. Likewise a love that one may have entertained for anyone will not be forgotten in the world of the Kingdom, nor wilt thou forget there the life that thou hadst in the material world.[27]

Beholding the Beauty of God

As to the question whether the souls will recognize each other in the spiritual world: This fact is certain; for the Kingdom is the world of vision where all the concealed realities will become disclosed. How much more the well-known souls will become manifest. The mysteries of which man is heedless in this earthly world, those he will discover in the heavenly world, and there will he be informed of the secret of truth; how much more will he recognize or discover persons with whom he hath been associated. Undoubtedly, the holy souls who find a pure eye and are favored with insight will, in the kingdom of light, be acquainted with all mysteries, and will seek the bounty of witnessing the reality of every great soul. Even they will manifestly behold the Beauty of God in that world. Likewise will they find all the friends of God, both those of the former and recent times, present in the heavenly assemblage.[28]

Discoveries to Come

Thou didst write as to the question of spiritual discoveries. The spirit of man is a circumambient power that encompasseth the realities of all things. Whatsoever thou dost see about thee—wondrous products of human workmanship, inventions, discoveries and like evidences—each one of these was once a secret hidden away in the realm of the unknown. The human spirit laid that secret bare, and drew it forth from the unseen into the visible world. There is, for example, the power of steam, and photography and the phonograph, and wireless telegraphy, and advances in mathematics: each and every one of these was once a mystery, a closely guarded secret, yet the human spirit unraveled these secrets and brought them out of the invisible into the light of day. Thus is it clear that the human spirit is an all-encompassing power that exerteth its dominion over the inner essences of all created things, uncovering the well kept mysteries of the phenomenal world.

The divine spirit, however, doth unveil divine realities and universal mysteries that lie within the spiritual world. It is my hope that thou wilt attain unto this divine spirit, so that thou mayest uncover the secrets of the other world, as well as the mysteries of the world below.[29]

Discoveries to Come

As to thy question regarding discoveries made by the soul after it hath put off its human form: certainly, that world is a world of perceptions and discoveries, for the interposed veil will be lifted away and the human spirit will gaze upon souls that are above, below, and on a par with itself. It is similar to the condition of a human being in the womb, where his eyes are veiled, and all things are hidden away from him. Once he is born out of the uterine world and entereth this life, he findeth it, with relation to that of the womb, to be a place of perceptions and discoveries, and he observeth all things through his outer eye. In the same way, once he hath departed this life, he will behold, in that world whatsoever was hidden from him here: but there he will look upon and comprehend all things with his inner eye. There will he gaze on his fellows and his peers, and those in the ranks above him, and those below.[30]

* * *

Consider how a being, in the world of the womb, was deaf of ear and blind of eye, and mute of tongue; how he was bereft of any perceptions at all. But once, out of that world of darkness, he passed into this world of light, then his eye saw, his ear heard, his tongue spoke. In the same way, once he hath hastened away from this mortal place into the Kingdom of God, then he will be born in the spirit; then the eye of his perception will open, the ear of his soul will hearken, and all the truths of which he was ignorant before will be made plain and clear.

An observant traveler passing along a way will certainly recall his discoveries to mind, unless some accident befall him and efface the memory.[31]

Tampering With Psychic Forces

To tamper with psychic forces while in this world interferes with the condition of the soul in the world to come. These forces are real, but, normally, are not active on this plane. The child in the womb has its eyes, ears, hands, feet, etc., but they are not in activity. The whole purpose of life in the material world is the coming forth into the world of Reality, where those forces will become active. They belong to that world.[32]

Conversing With the Departed

"Can a departed soul converse with someone still on earth?"

'Abdu'l-Bahá: "A conversation can be held, but not as our conversation. There is no doubt that the forces of the higher worlds interplay with the forces of this plane. The heart of man is open to inspiration; this is spiritual communication. As in a dream one talks with a friend while the mouth is silent, so is it in the conversation of the spirit. A man may converse with the ego within him saying: 'May I do this? Would it be advisable for me to do this work?' Such as this is conversation with the higher self."[33]

Communication With Holy Souls

When the souls leave the bodies, they do not assume elemental bodies. Whatever man thinks regarding this is but his own imagination.

When man desires help and communication from holy souls, he puts himself in a condition of self-unconsciousness and becomes submerged in the sea of meditation, then a spiritual state, which is sanctified from matter and all material things, becomes visible and apparent to him. Then he thinks he beholds a form. Its appearance is like unto a vision.

Man beholds in the world of vision various images, communicates with them, and receives benefits, and in that world of vision he *thinks* they are physical temples and material bodies, while they are purely *immaterial.*

Briefly, the reality of the soul is sanctified and purified above matter and material things, but like unto the world of vision, it manifests itself in these material forms and visages. Likewise, in the psychic condition, one beholds the spirits like unto physical forms and visages.

To be brief, the holy souls have great influence and intense effect, and their influence and continuity does not depend upon physical existence and elemental composition.

Ponder ye, that during sleep the human body and the five physical senses, viz., sight, smell, taste, hearing, and touch are passive—i.e., all physical forces are inactive. Notwithstanding this, human reality has spiritual life, and the spiritual powers are penetrative; and wonderful disclosures are made in both the East and the West, and perchance one may discover some matters, which, after a long time, may become apparent in the physical world. Therefore, it has become evident that the continuity and influence of the human reality does not depend upon the physical instrumentality; nay, rather, the physical body is an instrument over which the human spirit spreads a luminosity. It is like unto the sun which, shining upon the mirror, causes its brilliancy, and when the reflection is withdrawn from the mirror, it becomes dark. Likewise, when the luminosity of the human spirit is withdrawn from the body, that instrument becomes useless.

To be brief, Humanity consists of the spiritual reality, and that reality is penetrative in all things, and it is that reality which discovers the invisible mysteries, and through that reality all sciences, arts, and inventions become known and manifest. Whatever thou beholdest of the worlds of man is but a faint ray of that reality. It encircles all things and comprehends all things.

Reflect thou that all these existent sciences, crafts, industries, and arts were at one time in the world of invisibility, unknown and concealed mysteries. As the spirit of man environs all things, therefore he has discovered them and brought them from the unknown world into the arena of manifestation.

Therefore, it is evident and established that the human spirit is the discoverer of things, the seer of things, and the comprehender of things.[34]

Visions and Communication With Spirits

Question: Some people believe that they achieve spiritual discoveries—that is to say, that they converse with spirits. What kind of communion is this?

Answer: Spiritual discoveries are of two kinds: one kind is of the imagination and is only the assertion of a few people; the other kind resembles inspiration, and this is real—such are the revelations of Isaiah, of Jeremiah and of St. John, which are real.

Reflect that man's power of thought consists of two kinds. One kind is true, when it agrees with a determined truth. Such conceptions find realization in the exterior world; such are accurate opinions, correct theories, scientific discoveries and inventions.

The other kind of conceptions is made up of vain thoughts and useless ideas which yield neither fruit nor result, and which have no reality. No, they surge like the waves of the sea of imaginations, and they pass away like idle dreams.

In the same way, there are two sorts of spiritual discoveries. One is the revelations of the Prophets, and the spiritual discoveries of the elect. The visions of the Prophets are not dreams; no, they are spiritual discoveries and have reality. They say, for example, "I saw a person in a certain form, and I said such a thing, and he gave such an answer." This vision is in the world of wakefulness, and not in that of sleep. Nay, it is a spiritual discovery which is expressed as if it were the appearance of a vision.

The other kind of spiritual discoveries is made up of pure imaginations, but these imaginations become embodied in such a way that many simple-hearted people believe that they have a reality. That which proves it clearly is that from this controlling of spirits no result or fruit has ever been produced. No, they are but narratives and stories.

Know that the reality of man embraces the realities of things, and discovers the verities, properties and secrets of things. So all these arts, wonders, sciences and knowledge have been discovered by the human reality. At one time these sciences, knowledge, wonders and arts were hidden and concealed secrets; then gradually the human reality discovered them and brought them from the realm of the invisible to the plane of the visible. Therefore, it is evident that the reality of man embraces things. Thus it is in Europe and discovers America; it is on the earth, and it makes discoveries in the heavens. It is the revealer of the secrets of things, and it is the knower of the realities of that which exists. These discoveries corresponding to the reality are similar to revelation, which is spiritual comprehension, divine inspiration and the association of human spirits. For instance, the Prophet says, "I saw, I said, I heard such a thing." It is, therefore, evident that the spirit has great perception without the intermediary of any of the five senses, such as the eyes or ears. Among spiritual souls there are spiritual understandings, discoveries, a communion which is purified from imagination and fancy, an association which is sanctified from time and place. So it is written in the Gospel that, on Mount Tabor, Moses and Elias came to Christ, and it is evident that this was not a material meeting. It was a spiritual condition which is expressed as a physical meeting.

The other sort of converse, presence and communications of spirits is but imagination and fancy, which only appears to have reality.

The mind and the thought of man sometimes discover truths, and from this thought and discovery signs and results are produced. This thought has a foundation. But many things come to the mind of man which are like the waves of the sea of imaginations; they have no fruit, and no result comes from them. In the same way, man sees in the world of sleep a vision which becomes exactly realized; at another time, he sees a dream which has absolutely no result.

What we mean is that this state, which we call the converse and communications of spirits, is of two kinds: one is simply imaginary, and the other is like the visions which are mentioned in the Holy Book, such as the revelations of St. John and Isaiah and the meeting of Christ with Moses and Elias. These are real, and produce wonderful effects in the minds and thoughts of men, and cause their hearts to be attracted.[35]

Receiving Messages From the Departed

Question: ...is it possible for persons to receive messages or trumpet communications from departed souls, etc.?

O, thou maidservant of God! There is a wonderful power and strength which belongs to the human spirit, but it must receive confirmation from the Holy Spirit. The rest of which you hear is superstition. But if it is aided by the Bounty of the Holy Spirit, it will show great power; it will discover realities; it will be informed of the mysteries. Direct all the attention to the Holy Spirit, and call the attention of every soul to It. Then will you see wonderful signs.

...Outside of the Bounty of the Holy Spirit all that thou hearest concerning mesmerism or trumpet communications from the dead are sheer imagination.

But thou canst say whatever thou desirest concerning the Bounty of the Holy Spirit, and what thou hearest from the Holy Spirit and obey. But the people who are mentioned, those in connection with the trumpets, are entirely bereft of this Bounty, and they have no portion therein. Theirs is imagination.[36]

Souls Can Influence Us

When you do not know it, and are in a receptive attitude, they are able to make suggestions to you, if you are in difficulty. This sometimes happens in sleep.[37]

Mediums

Regarding the materialization of spirits through mediums: A person finding himself in a state of trance, or unconsciousness, is like one who sleeps; whatever he feels and sees he imagines to be matter and of material things, but in reality they are wholly immaterial.[38]

Mediums and Trances

Outside the bounty of the Holy Spirit, whatsoever thou hearest as to the effect of trances, or the mediums' trumpets, conveying the singing voices of the dead, is imagination pure and simple. As to the bounty of the Holy Spirit however, relate whatsoever thou wilt—it cannot be overstated; believe, therefore, whatsoever thou hearest of this. But the persons referred to, the trumpet-people, are entirely shut out from this bounty and receive no portion thereof; their way is an illusion.[39]

Influence of Evil Spirits

You have asked regarding the influence of evil spirits. Evil spirits are deprived of eternal life. How then can they exercise any influence? But as *eternal life* is ordained for holy spirits, therefore their influence exists in all the divine worlds.

At the time you were here, this question was accordingly answered, that after the ascension of the godly souls, great influence and widespreading bounties are destined for them, and all-encircling signs in the seen and unseen are decreed for them.[40]

No Real Separation Between Departed and Living

Those who have ascended have different attributes from those who are still on earth, yet there is no real separation.

In prayer there is a mingling of station, a mingling of condition. Pray for them as they pray for you![41]

That World Within This World

...the center of the Sun of Truth is in the supernal world—the Kingdom of God. Those souls who are pure and unsullied, upon the dissolution of their elemental frames, hasten away to the world of God, and that world is within this world.

The people of this world, however, are unaware of that world, and are even as the mineral and the vegetable that know nothing of the world of the animal and the world of man.[42]

The True Believer in Touch With the Heavenly Kingdom

Those souls that, in this day, enter the divine kingdom and attain everlasting life, although materially dwelling on earth, yet in reality soar in the realm of heaven. Their bodies may linger on earth but their spirits travel in the immensity of space. For as thoughts widen and become illumined, they acquire the power of flight and transport man to the kingdom of God.[43]

Mediators of God's Power

When 'Abdu'l-Bahá was asked how it was that the heart often turns with instinctive appeal to some friend who has passed into the next life, He answered: "It is a law of God's creation that the weak should lean upon the strong. Those to whom you turn may be mediators of God's power to you, even as when on earth. But it is the One Holy Spirit that strengthens all men."[44]

Teaching the Departed Souls

Asked whether it was possible through faith and love to bring the New Revelation to the knowledge of those who have departed from this life without hearing of it, 'Abdu'l-Bahá replied: "Yes, surely! since sincere prayer always has its effect, and it has a great influence in the other world. We are never cut off from those who are there. The real and genuine influence is not in this world but in that other."[45]

True Unity Between Spouses Everlasting

When relationship, union and concord exist between the two from a physical and spiritual standpoint, that is the real union, therefore everlasting. But if the union is merely from the physical point of view, unquestionably it is temporal and at the end separation is inevitable.[46]

* * *

The marriage of the Bahá'ís means that both man and woman must become spiritually and physically united, so that they may have eternal unity throughout all the divine worlds and improve the spiritual life of each other. This is Bahá'í matrimony...

The souls who sacrifice self, become detached from the perfections of the realm of man and free from the shackles of this ephemeral world, assuredly the splendors of the rays of divine union shall shine in their hearts and in the eternal paradise they shall find ideal relationship, union and happiness.[47]

Power of the Spirit in the Body

Verily, I say unto thee that the gifts of thy Lord are encircling thee in a similar way as the spirit encircles the body at the beginning of the amalgamation of the elements and natures in the womb; the power of the spirit begins then to appear in the body gradually and successively according to the preparation and capacity to receive that everlasting abundance.[48]

Death of Children

Question: What is the condition of children who die before attaining the age of discretion or before the appointed time of birth?

Answer: These infants are under the shadow of the favor of God; and as they have not committed any sin and are not soiled with the impurities of the world of nature, they are the centers of the manifestation of bounty, and the Eye of Compassion will be turned upon them.[49]

Reasons For Early Deaths

As to the subject of babes and infants and weak ones who are afflicted by the hands of oppressors: This contains great wisdom and this subject is of paramount importance. In brief, for those souls there is a recompense in another world and many details are connected with this matter. For those souls that suffering is the greatest mercy of God. Verily that mercy of the Lord is far better and preferable to all the comfort of this world and the growth and development of this place of mortality.[50]

The Abode of the Children of the Kingdom

...the souls of the children of the Kingdom, after their separation from the body, ascend unto the realm of everlasting life. But if ye ask as to the place, know ye that the world of existence is a single world, although its stations are various and distinct. For example, the mineral life occupieth its own plane, but a mineral entity is without any awareness at all of the vegetable kingdom, and indeed, with its inner tongue denieth that there is any such kingdom. In the same way, a vegetable entity knoweth nothing of the animal world, remaining completely heedless and ignorant thereof, for the stage of the animal is higher than that of the vegetable, and the vegetable is veiled from the animal world and inwardly denieth the existence of that world—all this while animal, vegetable and mineral dwell together in the one world. In the same way the animal remaineth totally unaware of that power of the human mind which graspeth universal ideas and layeth bare the secrets of creation—so that a man who liveth in the east can make plans and arrangements for the west; can unravel mysteries; although located on the continent of Europe can discover America; although sited on the earth can lay hold of the inner realities of the stars of heaven. Of this power of discovery which belongeth to the human mind, this power which can grasp abstract and universal ideas, the animal remaineth totally ignorant, and indeed denieth its existence.

In the same way, the denizens of this earth are completely unaware of the world of the Kingdom and deny the existence thereof. They ask, for example: 'where is the Kingdom? Where is the Lord of the Kingdom?' These people are even as the mineral and the vegetable, who know nothing whatever of the animal and the human realm; they see it not; they find it not. Yet the mineral and vegetable, the animal and man, are all living here together in this world of existence.[51]

Every Soul Born Pure

Know thou that every soul is fashioned after the nature of God, each being pure and holy at his birth. Afterwards, however, the individuals will vary according to what they acquire of virtues or vices in this world. Although all existent beings are in their very nature created in ranks or degrees, for capacities are various, nevertheless every individual is born holy and pure, and only thereafter may he become defiled.

And further, although the degrees of being are various, yet all are good. Observe the human body, its limbs, its members, the eye, the ear, the organs of smell, of taste, the hands, the finger-nails. Notwithstanding the differences among all these parts, each one within the limitations of its own being participateth in a coherent whole. If one of them faileth it must be healed, and should no remedy avail, that part must be removed.[52]

Residents of the Supreme Concourse

...another friend referred to the communing of Jesus on the Mount of Transfiguration with Moses and Elijah; and 'Abdu'l-Bahá said: "The faithful are ever sustained by the presence of the Supreme Concourse. In the Supreme Concourse are Jesus, and Moses, and Elijah, and Bahá'u'lláh, and other supreme Souls: there, also, are the martyrs."[53]

Meaning of "Angels"

The meaning of 'angels' is the confirmations of God and His celestial powers. Likewise angels are blessed beings who have severed all ties with this nether world, have been released from the chains of self and the desires of the flesh, and anchored their hearts to the heavenly realms of the Lord. These are of the Kingdom, heavenly; these are of God, spiritual; these are revealers of God's abounding grace; these are dawning-points of His spiritual bestowals.[54]

Heaven and Hell

Now punishments and rewards are said to be of two kinds: first, the rewards and punishments of this life; second, those of the other world. But the paradise and hell of existence are found in all the worlds of God, whether in this world or in the spiritual heavenly worlds. Gaining these rewards is the gaining of eternal life. That is why Christ said, "Act in such a way that you may find eternal life, and that you may be born of water and the spirit, so that you may enter into the Kingdom."*

The rewards of this life are the virtues and perfections which adorn the reality of man. For example, he was dark and becomes luminous; he was ignorant and becomes wise; he was neglectful and becomes vigilant; he was asleep and becomes awakened; he was dead and becomes living; he was blind and becomes a seer; he was deaf and becomes a hearer; he was earthly and becomes heavenly; he was material and becomes spiritual. Through these rewards he gains spiritual birth and becomes a new creature. He becomes the manifestation of the verse in the Gospel where it is said of the disciples that they "were born, not of blood, nor of the will of the flesh, nor of the will of man, but of God"*—that is to say, they were delivered from the animal characteristics and qualities which are the characteristics of human nature, and they became qualified with the divine characteristics, which are the bounty of God. This is the meaning of the second birth. For such people there is no greater torture than being veiled from God, and no more severe punishment than sensual vices, dark qualities, lowness of nature, engrossment in carnal desires. When they are delivered through the light of faith from the darkness of these vices, and become illuminated with the radiance of the sun of reality, and ennobled with all the virtues, they esteem this the greatest reward, and they know it to be the true paradise. In the same way they consider that the spiritual punishment—that is to say, the torture and punishment of existence—is to be subjected to the world of nature; to be veiled from God; to be brutal and ignorant; to fall into carnal lusts; to be absorbed in animal frailties; to be characterized with dark qualities, such as falsehood, tyranny, cruelty, attachment to the affairs of the world, and being immersed in satanic ideas. For them, these are the greatest punishments and tortures.

Likewise, the rewards of the other world are the eternal life which is clearly mentioned in all the Holy Books, the divine

---

*John 3:5.
*John 1:13.

perfections, the eternal bounties and everlasting felicity. The rewards of the other world are the perfections and the peace obtained in the spiritual worlds after leaving this world, while the rewards of this life are the real luminous perfections which are realized in this world, and which are the cause of eternal life, for they are the very progress of existence. It is like the man who passes from the embryonic world to the state of maturity and becomes the manifestation of these words: "Blessed, therefore, be God, the most excellent of Makers."* The rewards of the other world are peace, the spiritual graces, the various spiritual gifts in the Kingdom of God, the gaining of the desires of the heart and the soul, and the meeting of God in the world of eternity. In the same way the punishments of the other world—that is to say, the torments of the other world—consist in being deprived of the special divine blessings and the absolute bounties, and falling into the lowest degrees of existence. He who is deprived of these divine favors, although he continues after death, is considered as dead by the people of truth.[55]

Symbolic Descriptions in Qur'án and Gospel

Relative to the Paradise explained by Muhammad in the Qur'án, such utterances are spiritual and are cast into the mold of words and figures of speech; for at that time people did not possess the capacity of comprehending spiritual significances. It is similar to that reference to His Highness Christ who, addressing His disciples said, "I shall not partake of the fruit of the vine anymore until I reach the Kingdom of My Father." Now it is evident His Highness Christ did not mean material grapes, but it was a spiritual condition and a heavenly state which He interpreted as this fruit.

Now, whatever is revealed in the Qur'án has the same import.[56]

---

*Qur'án 23:14.

The Human Form in the Afterlife

...in the other world the human reality doth not assume a physical form, rather doth it take on a heavenly form, made up of elements of that heavenly realm.[57]

No Tests or Trials in the Next Life

...the tests and trials of God take place in this world, not in the world of the Kingdom.[58]

Those Who Are Deprived in This Life

As to those souls who are born into this life as ethereal and radiant entities and yet, on account of their handicaps and trials, are deprived of great and real advantages, and leave the world without having lived to the full—certainly this is a cause for grieving. This is the reason why the universal Manifestations of God unveil Their countenances to man, and endure every calamity and sore affliction, and lay down Their lives as a ransom; it is to make these very people, the ready ones, the ones who have capacity, to become dawning points of light, and to bestow upon them the life that fadeth never. This is the true sacrifice: the offering of oneself, even as did Christ, as a ransom for the life of the world.[59]

Everything Happens For a Reason

Today I have been speaking from dawn until now, yet because of love, fellowship and desire to be with you, I have come here to speak again briefly. Within the last few days a terrible event has happened in the world, an event saddening to every heart and grieving every spirit. I refer to the *Titanic* disaster, in which many of our fellow human beings were drowned, a number of beautiful souls passed beyond this earthly life. Although such an event is indeed regrettable, we must realize that everything which happens is due to some wisdom and that nothing happens without a reason. Therein is a mystery; but whatever the reason and mystery, it was a very sad occurrence, one which brought tears to many eyes and distress to many souls. I was greatly affected by this disaster. Some of those who were lost voyaged on the *Cedric* with us as far as Naples and afterward sailed upon the other ship. When I think of them, I am very sad indeed. But when I consider this calamity in another aspect, I am consoled by the realization that the worlds of God are infinite; that though they were deprived of this existence, they have other opportunities in the life beyond, even as Christ has said, "In my Father's house are many mansions." They were called away from the temporary and transferred to the eternal; they abandoned this material existence and entered the portals of the spiritual world. Foregoing the pleasures and comforts of the earthly, they now partake of a joy and happiness far more abiding and real, for they have hastened to the Kingdom of God. The mercy of God is infinite, and it is our duty to remember these departed souls in our prayers and supplications that they may draw nearer and nearer to the Source itself.

These human conditions may be likened to the matrix of the mother from which a child is to be born into the spacious outer world. At first the infant finds it very difficult to reconcile itself to its new existence. It cries as if not wishing to be separated from its narrow abode and imagining that life is restricted to that limited space. It is reluctant to leave its home, but nature forces it into this world. Having come into its new conditions, it finds that it has passed from darkness into a sphere of radiance; from gloomy and restricted surroundings it has been transferred to a spacious and delightful environment. Its nourishment was the blood of the mother; now it finds delicious food to enjoy. Its new life is filled with brightness and beauty; it looks with wonder and delight upon the mountains, meadows and fields of green, the rivers and fountains, the wonderful stars; it breathes the life-quickening atmosphere; and then it praises God for its release from the confinement of its former condition and attainment to the freedom of a new realm. This analogy expresses the relation of the temporal world to the life hereafter—the transition of the soul of man from darkness and uncertainty to the light and reality of the eternal Kingdom. At first it is very difficult to welcome death, but after attaining its new condition the soul is grateful, for it has been released from the bondage of the limited to enjoy the liberties of the unlimited. It has been freed from a world of sorrow, grief and trials to live in a world of unending bliss and joy. The phenomenal and physical have been abandoned in order that it may attain the opportunities of the ideal and spiritual. Therefore, the souls of those who have passed away from earth and completed their span of mortal pilgrimage in the *Titanic* disaster have hastened to a world superior to this. They have soared away from these conditions of darkness and dim vision into the realm of light. These are the only considerations which can comfort and console those whom they have left behind.

Furthermore, these events have deeper reasons. Their object and purpose is to teach man certain lessons. We are living in a day of reliance upon material conditions. Men imagine that the great size and strength of a ship, the perfection of machinery or the skill of a navigator will ensure safety, but these disasters sometimes take place that men may know that God is the real Protector. If it be the will of God to protect man, a little ship may escape destruction, whereas the greatest and most perfectly constructed vessel with the best and most skillful navigator may not survive a danger such as was present on the ocean. The purpose is that the people of the world may turn to God, the One Protector; that human souls may rely upon His preservation and know that He is the real safety. These events happen in order that man's faith may be increased and strengthened. Therefore, although we feel sad and disheartened, we must supplicate

God to turn our hearts to the Kingdom and pray for these departed souls with faith in His infinite mercy so that, although they have been deprived of this earthly life, they may enjoy a new existence in the supreme mansions of the Heavenly Father.

Let no one imagine that these words imply that man should not be thorough and careful in his undertakings. God has endowed man with intelligence so that he may safeguard and protect himself. Therefore, he must provide and surround himself with all that scientific skill can produce. He must be deliberate, thoughtful and thorough in his purposes, build the best ship and provide the most experienced captain; yet, withal, let him rely upon God and consider God as the one Keeper. If God protects, nothing can imperil man's safety; and if it be not His will to safeguard, no amount of preparation and precaution will avail.[60]

On the Death of a Youth

The death of that beloved youth and his separation from you have caused the utmost sorrow and grief; for he winged his flight in the flower of his age and the bloom of his youth to the heavenly nest. But he hath been freed from this sorrow-stricken shelter and hath turned his face toward the everlasting nest of the Kingdom, and, being delivered from a dark and narrow world, hath hastened to the sanctified realm of light; therein lieth the consolation of our hearts.

The inscrutable divine wisdom underlieth such heart-rending occurrences. It is as if a kind gardener transferreth a fresh and tender shrub from a confined place to a wide open area. This transfer is not the cause of the withering, the lessening or the destruction of that shrub; nay, on the contrary, it maketh it to grow and thrive, acquire freshness and delicacy, become green and bear fruit. This hidden secret is well known to the gardener, but those souls who are unaware of this bounty suppose that the gardener, in his anger and wrath, hath uprooted the shrub. Yet to those who are aware, this concealed fact is manifest, and this predestined decree is considered a bounty. Do not feel grieved or disconsolate, therefore, at the ascension of that bird of faithfulness; nay, under all circumstances pray for that youth, supplicating for him forgiveness and the elevation of his station.

I hope that ye will attain the utmost patience, composure and resignation, and I entreat and implore at the Threshold of Oneness, begging for forgiveness and pardon. My hope from the infinite bounties of God is that He may shelter this dove of the garden of faith, and cause him to abide on the branch of the Supreme Concourse, that he may sing in the best of melodies the praise and glorification of the Lord of Names and Attributes.[61]

On the Sudden Death of a Beloved Disciple

Grieve thou not over the ascension of my beloved Breakwell, for he hath risen unto a rose garden of splendors within the Abhá [the Most Glorious] Paradise, sheltered by the mercy of his mighty Lord, and he is crying at the top of his voice: 'O that my people could know how graciously my Lord hath forgiven me, and made me to be of those who have attained His Presence!'

O Breakwell, O my dear one!
Where now is thy fair face? Where is thy fluent tongue? Where thy clear brow? Where thy bright comeliness?

O Breakwell, O my dear one!
Where is thy fire, blazing with God's love? Where is thy rapture at His holy breaths? Where are thy praises, lifted unto Him? Where is thy rising up to serve His Cause?

O Breakwell, O my dear one!
Where are thy beauteous eyes? Thy smiling lips? The princely cheek? The graceful form?

O Breakwell, O my dear one!
Thou hast quit this earthly world and risen upward to the Kingdom, thou hast reached unto the grace of the invisible realm, and offered thyself at the threshold of its Lord.

O Breakwell, O my dear one!
Thou hast left the lamp that was thy body here, the glass that was thy human form, thy earthy elements, thy way of life below.

O Breakwell, O my dear one!
Thou hast lit a flame within the lamp of the Company on high, thou hast set foot in the Abhá Paradise, thou hast found a shelter in the shadow of the Blessed Tree, thou hast attained His meeting in the haven of Heaven.

O Breakwell, O my dear one!
Thou art now a bird of Heaven, thou hast quit thine earthly nest, and soared away to a garden of holiness in the kingdom of thy Lord. Thou hast risen to a station filled with light.

O Breakwell, O my dear one!
Thy song is even as birdsong now, thou pourest forth verses as to the mercy of thy Lord; of Him Who forgiveth ever, thou wert a thankful servant, wherefore hast thou entered into exceeding bliss.

O Breakwell, O my dear one!
Thy Lord hath verily singled thee out for His love, and hath led thee into His precincts of holiness, and made thee to enter the garden of those who are His close companions, and hath blessed thee with beholding His beauty.

O Breakwell, O my dear one!
Thou hast won eternal life, and the bounty that faileth never, and a life to please thee well, and plenteous grace.

O Breakwell, O my dear one!
Thou art become a star in the supernal sky, and a lamp amid the angels of high Heaven; a living spirit in the most exalted Kingdom, throned in eternity.

O Breakwell, O my dear one!
I ask of God to draw thee ever closer, hold thee ever faster; to rejoice thy heart with nearness to His presence, to fill

thee with light and still more light, to grant thee still more beauty, and to bestow upon thee power and great glory.

O Breakwell, O my dear one!
At all times do I call thee to mind. I shall never forget thee. I pray for thee by day, by night; I see thee plain before me, as if in open day.

O Breakwell, O my dear one![62]

On the Death of a Spouse

O thou assured soul, thou maidservant of God... Be not grieved at the death of thy respected husband. He hath, verily, attained the meeting of His Lord at the seat of Truth in the presence of the potent King. Do not suppose that thou hast lost him. The veil shall be lifted and thou shalt behold his face illumined in the Supreme Concourse. Just as God, the Exalted, hath said, 'Him will we surely quicken to a happy life.' Supreme importance should be attached, therefore, not to this first creation but rather to the future life.[63]

* * *

O thou seeker of the Kingdom! Thy letter was received. Thou hast written of the severe calamity that hath befallen thee—the death of thy respected husband. That honorable man hath been so subjected to the stress and strain of this world that his greatest wish was for deliverance from it. Such is this mortal abode: a storehouse of afflictions and suffering. It is ignorance that binds man to it, for no comfort can be secured by any soul in this world, from monarch down to the most humble commoner. If once this life should offer a man a sweet cup, a hundred bitter ones will follow; such is the condition of this world. The wise man, therefore, doth not attach himself to this mortal life and doth not depend upon it; at some moments, even, he eagerly wisheth for death that he may thereby be freed from these sorrows and afflictions. Thus it is seen that some, under extreme pressure of anguish, have committed suicide.

As to thy husband, rest assured. He will be immersed in the ocean of pardon and forgiveness and will become the recipient of bounty and favor. Strive thine utmost to give his child a Bahá'í training so that when he attaineth maturity he may be merciful, illumined and heavenly.[64]

On the Death of a Child

O thou beloved maid-servant of God, although the loss of a son is indeed heart-breaking and beyond the limits of human endurance, yet one who knoweth and understandeth is assured that the son hath not been lost but, rather, hath stepped from this world into another, and she will find him in the divine realm. That reunion shall be for eternity, while in this world separation is inevitable and bringeth with it a burning grief.

Praise be unto God that thou hast faith, art turning thy face toward the everlasting Kingdom and believest in the existence of a heavenly world. Therefore be thou not disconsolate, do not languish, do not sigh, neither wail nor weep; for agitation and mourning deeply affect his soul in the divine realm.

That beloved child addresseth thee from the hidden world: 'O thou kind Mother, thank divine Providence that I have been freed from a small and gloomy cage and, like the birds of the meadows, have soared to the divine world—a world which is spacious, illumined, and ever gay and jubilant. Therefore, lament not, O Mother, and be not grieved; I am not of the lost, nor have I been obliterated and destroyed. I have shaken off the mortal form and have raised my banner in this spiritual world. Following this separation is everlasting companionship. Thou shalt find me in the heaven of the Lord, immersed in an ocean of light.'[65]

'Abdu'l-Bahá's Dream of a Disciple Who Had Departed to the Next Kingdom

I loved him [Mullá Alí-Akbar] very much, for he was delight-ful to converse with, and as a companion second to none. One night, not long ago, I saw him in the world of dreams. Although his frame had always been massive, in the dream world he appeared larger and more corpulent than ever. It seemed as if he had returned from a journey. I said to him, "Jináb, you have grown good and stout." "Yes," he answered, "praise be to God! I have been in places where the air was fresh and sweet, and the water crystal pure; the landscapes were beautiful to look upon, the foods delectable. It all agreed with me, of course, so I am stronger than ever now, and I have recovered the zest of my early youth. The breaths of the All-Merciful blew over me and all my time was spent in telling of God. I have been setting forth His proofs, and teaching His Faith." (The meaning of teaching the Faith in the next world is spreading the sweet savors of holiness; that action is the same as teaching.) We spoke together a little more, and then some people arrived and he disappeared.[66]

Accountability of Leaders in the Next Kingdom

By the All-Glorious! I am astonished to find what a veil has fallen across their eyes, and how it blinds them even to such obvious necessities as these. And there is no doubt whatever that when conclusive arguments and proofs of this sort are advanced, they will answer, out of a thousand hidden spites and prejudices: "On the Day of Judgment, when men stand before their Lord, they will not be questioned as to their education and the degree of their culture—rather will they be examined as to their good deeds." Let us grant this and assume that man will not be asked as to his culture and education; even so, on that great Day of Reckoning, will not the leaders be called to account? Will it not be said to them: "O chiefs and leaders! Why did ye cause this mighty nation to fall from the heights of its former glory, to pass from its place at the heart and center of the civilized world? Ye were well able to take hold of such measures as would lead to the high honor of this people. This ye failed to do, and ye even went on to deprive them of the common benefits enjoyed by all. Did not this people once shine out like stars in an auspicious heaven? How have ye dared to quench their light in darkness! Ye could have lit the lamp of temporal and eternal glory for them; why did ye fail to strive for this with all your hearts? And when by God's grace a flaming Light flared up, why did ye fail to shelter it in the glass of your valor, from the winds that beat against it? Why did ye rise up in all your might to put it out?"

"And every man's fate have We fastened about his neck: and on the Day of Resurrection will We bring it forth to him a book which shall be proffered to him wide open."[67]

The Meaning of "Return"

Now as to what thou askest concerning the spirit and its "return" to this world of humanity and this elemental space: Know that spirit in general is divided into five sorts—the vegetable spirit, the animal spirit, the human spirit, the spirit of faith, and the divine spirit of sanctity.

The vegetable spirit is the virtue augmentative, or growing or vegetative faculty, which results from the admixture of the simple elements, with the cooperation of water, air and heat.

The animal spirit is the virtue perceptive resulting from the admixture and absorption of the vital elements generated in the heart, which apprehend sense-impressions.

The human spirit consists of the rational, or logical, reasoning faculty, which apprehends general ideas and things intelligible and perceptible.

Now these "spirits" are not reckoned as Spirit in the terminology of the Scriptures and the usage of the people of the Truth, inasmuch as the laws governing them are as the laws which govern all phenomenal being in respect to generation, corruption, production, change and reversion, as is clearly indicated in the Gospel where it says: "Let the dead bury their dead"; "That which is born of the flesh is flesh, and that which is born of the Spirit is Spirit"; inasmuch as he who would bury these dead was alive with the vegetative, animal and rational human soul, yet did Christ—to whom be glory!—declare such dead and devoid of life, in that this person was devoid of the spirit of faith, which is of the Kingdom of God.

In brief, for these three spirits there is no restitution or "return," but they are subordinate to reversions and production and corruption.

But the spirit of faith which is of the Kingdom consists of the all-comprehending grace and the perfect attainment and the power of sanctity and the divine effulgence from the Sun of Truth on luminous light-seeking essences from the presence of the divine Unity. And by this Spirit is the life of the spirit of man, when it is fortified thereby, as Christ saith: "That which is born of the Spirit is Spirit." And this Spirit hath both restitution and return, inasmuch as it consists of the Light of God and the unconditioned grace. So, having regard to this state and station, Christ announced that John the Baptist was Elias, who was to come before Christ. And the likeness of this station is as that of lamps kindled: for these in respect to their glasses and oil-holders, are different, but in respect to their light, One, and in respect to their illumination, One; nay, each one is identical with the other, without imputation of plurality, or diversity or multiplicity or separateness. This is the Truth and beyond the Truth there is only error.[68]

Reincarnation (I)

Thou didst write of reincarnation. A belief in reincarnation goeth far back into the ancient history of almost all peoples, and was held even by the philosophers of Greece, the Roman sages, the ancient Egyptians, and the great Assyrians. Nevertheless such superstitions and sayings are but absurdities in the sight of God.

The major argument of the reincarnationists was this, that according to the justice of God, each must receive his due: whenever a man is afflicted with some calamity, for example, this is because of some wrong he hath committed. But take a child that is still in its mother's womb, the embryo but newly formed, and that child is blind, deaf, lame, defective—what sin hath such a child committed, to deserve its afflictions? They answer that, although to outward seeming the child, still in the womb, is guilty of no sin—nevertheless he perpetrated some wrong when in his previous form, and thus he came to deserve his punishment.

These individuals, however, have overlooked the following point. If creation went forward according to only one rule, how could the all-encompassing Power make Itself felt? How could the Almighty be the One Who 'doeth as He pleaseth and ordaineth as He willeth'?

Briefly, a return is indeed referred to in the Holy Scriptures, but by this is meant the return of the qualities, conditions, effects, perfections, and inner realities of the lights which recur in every dispensation. The reference is not to specific individual souls and identities.

It may be said, for instance, that this lamplight is last night's come back again, or that last year's rose hath returned to the garden this year. Here the reference is not to the individual reality, the fixed identity, the specialized being of that other rose, rather doth it mean that the qualities, the distinctive characteristics of that other light, that other flower, are present now, in these. Those perfections, that is, those graces and gifts of a former springtime are back again this year. We say, for example, that this fruit is the same as last year's; but we are thinking only of the delicacy, bloom and freshness, and the sweet taste of it; for it is obvious that that impregnable center of reality, that specific identity, can never return.

What peace, what ease and comfort did the Holy Ones of God ever discover during Their sojourn in this nether world, that They should continually seek to come back and live this life again? Doth not a single turn at this anguish, these afflictions, these calamities, these body blows, these dire straits, suffice, that They should wish for repeated visits to the life of this world? This cup was not so sweet that one would care to drink of it a second time.

Therefore do the lovers of the Abhá [the Most Glorious] Beauty wish for no other recompense but to reach that station where they may gaze upon Him in the Realm of Glory, and they walk no other path save over desert sand of longing for those exalted heights. They seek that ease and solace which will abide forever, and those bestowals that are sanctified beyond the understanding of the worldly mind.[69]

Reincarnation (II)

Question: What is the truth of the question of reincarnation, which is believed by some people?

Answer: The object of what we are about to say is to explain the reality—not to deride the beliefs of other people; it is only to explain the facts; that is all. We do not oppose anyone's ideas, nor do we approve of criticism.

Know, then, that those who believe in reincarnation are of two classes: one class does not believe in the spiritual punishments and rewards of the other world, and they suppose that man by reincarnation and return to this world gains rewards and recompenses; they consider heaven and hell to be restricted to this world and do not speak of the existence of the other world. Among these there are two further divisions. One division thinks that man sometimes returns to this world in the form of an animal in order to undergo severe punishment and that, after enduring this painful torment, he will be released from the animal world and will come again into the human world; this is called transmigration. The other division thinks that from the human world one again returns to the human world, and that by this return rewards and punishments for a former life are obtained; this is called reincarnation. Neither of these classes speak of any other world besides this one.

The second sort of believers in reincarnation affirm the existence of the other world, and they consider reincarnation the means of becoming perfect—that is, they think that man, by going from and coming again to this world, will gradually acquire perfections, until he reaches the inmost perfection. In other words, that men are composed of matter and force: matter in the beginning—that is to say, in the first cycle—is imperfect, but on coming repeatedly to this world it progresses and acquires refinement and delicacy, until it becomes like a polished mirror; and force, which is no other than spirit, is realized in it with all the perfections.

This is the presentation of the subject by those who believe in reincarnation and transmigration. We have condensed it; if we entered into the details, it would take much time. This summary is sufficient. No logical arguments and proofs of this question are brought forward; they are only suppositions and inferences from conjectures, and not conclusive arguments. Proofs must be asked for from the believers in reincarnation, and not conjectures, suppositions and imaginations.

But you have asked for arguments of the impossibility of reincarnation. This is what we must now explain. The first argument for its impossibility is that the outward is the expression of the inward; the earth is the mirror of the Kingdom; the material world corresponds to the spiritual world. Now observe that in the sensible world appearances are not repeated, for no being in any respect is identical with, nor the same as, another being. The sign of singleness is visible and apparent in all things. If all the granaries of the world were full of grain, you would not find two grains absolutely alike, the same and identical without any distinction. It is certain that there will be differences and distinctions between them. As the proof of uniqueness exists in all things, and the Oneness and Unity of God is apparent in the reality of all things, the repetition of the same appearance is absolutely impossible. Therefore, reincarnation, which is the repeated appearance of the same spirit with its former essence and condition in this same world of appearance, is impossible and unrealizable. As the repetition of the same appearance is impossible and interdicted for each of the material beings, so for spiritual beings also, a return to the same condition, whether in the arc of descent or in the arc of ascent, is interdicted and impossible, for the material corresponds to the spiritual.

Nevertheless, the return of material beings with regard to species is evident; so the trees which during former years brought forth leaves, blossoms and fruits in the coming years will bring forth exactly the same leaves, blossoms and fruits. This is called the repetition of species. If anyone makes an objection saying that the leaf, the blossom and the fruit have been decomposed, and have descended from the vegetable world to the mineral world, and again have come back from the mineral world to the vegetable world, and, therefore, there has been a repetition—the answer is that the blossom, the leaf and the fruit of last year were decomposed, and these combined elements were disintegrated and were dispersed in space, and that the particles of the leaf and fruit of last year, after decomposition, have not again become combined, and have not returned. On the contrary, by the composition of new elements, the species has returned. It is the same with the human body, which after decomposition becomes disintegrated, and the elements which composed it are dispersed. If, in like manner, this body should again return from the mineral or vegetable world, it would not have exactly the same composition of elements as the former man. Those elements have been decomposed and dispersed; they are dissipated in this vast space. Afterward, other particles of elements have been combined, and a second body has been formed; it may be that one of the particles of the former individual has entered into the composition of the succeeding individual, but these particles have not been conserved and kept, exactly and completely, without addition or diminution, so that they may be combined again, and from that composition and mingling another individual may come into existence. So it cannot be proved that this body with all its particles has returned; that the former man has become the latter; and that, consequently, there has been repetition; that the spirit also, like the body, has returned; and that after death its essence has come back to this world.

If we say that this reincarnation is for acquiring perfections so that matter may become refined and delicate, and that the light of the spirit may be manifest in it with the greatest perfection, this also is mere imagination. For, even supposing we believe in this argument, still change of nature is impossible through renewal and return. The essence of imperfection, by returning, does not become the reality of perfection; complete darkness, by returning, does not become the source of light; the essence of weakness is not transformed into power and might by returning, and an earthly nature does not become a heavenly reality. The tree of Zaqqúm [the infernal tree mentioned in the Qur'án], no matter how frequently it may come back, will not bring forth sweet fruit, and the good tree, no matter how often it may return, will not bear a bitter fruit. Therefore, it is evident that returning and coming back to the material world does not become the cause of perfection. This theory has no proofs nor evidences; it is simply an idea. No, in reality the cause of acquiring perfections is the bounty of God.

The Theosophists believe that man on the arc of ascent [of the Circle of Existence] will return many times until he reaches the Supreme Center; in that condition matter becomes a clear mirror, the light of the spirit will shine upon it with its full power, and essential perfection will be acquired. Now, this is an established and deep theological proposition, that the material worlds are terminated at the end of the arc of descent, and that the condition of man is at the end of the arc of descent, and at the beginning of the arc of ascent, which is opposite to the Supreme Center. Also, from the beginning to the end of the arc of ascent, there are numerous spiritual degrees. The arc of descent is called beginning [bringing forth], and that of ascent is called progress [producing something new]. The arc of descent ends in materialities, and the arc of ascent ends in spiritualities. The point of the compass in describing a circle makes no retrograde motion, for this would be contrary to the natural movement and the divine order; otherwise, the symmetry of the circle would be spoiled.

Moreover, this material world has not such value or such excellence that man, after having escaped from this cage, will desire a second time to fall into this snare. No, through the Eternal Bounty the worth and true ability of man becomes apparent and visible by traversing the degrees of existence, and not by returning. When the shell is once opened, it will be apparent and evident whether it contains a pearl or worthless matter. When once the plant has grown it will bring forth either thorns or flowers; there is no need for it to grow up again. Besides, advancing and moving in the worlds in a direct order according to the natural law is the cause of existence, and a movement contrary to the system and law of nature is the cause of nonexistence. The return of the soul after death is contrary to the natural movement, and opposed to the divine system.

Therefore, by returning, it is absolutely impossible to obtain existence; it is as if man, after being freed from the womb, should return to it a second time. Consider what a puerile imagination this is which is implied by the belief in reincarnation and transmigration. Believers in it consider the body as a vessel in which the spirit is contained, as water is contained in a cup; this water has been taken from one cup and poured into another. This is child's play.

They do not realize that the spirit is an incorporeal being, and does not enter and come forth, but is only connected with the body as the sun is with the mirror. If it were thus, and the spirit by returning to this material world could pass through the degrees and attain to essential perfection, it would be better if God prolonged the life of the spirit in the material world until it had acquired perfections and graces; it then would not be necessary for it to taste of the cup of death, or to acquire a second life.

The idea that existence is restricted to this perishable world, and the denial of the existence of divine worlds, originally proceeded from the imaginations of certain believers in reincarnation; but the divine worlds are infinite. If the divine worlds culminated in this material world, creation would be futile: nay, existence would be pure child's play. The result of these endless beings, which is the noble existence of man, would come and go for a few days in this perishable dwelling, and after receiving punishments and rewards, at last all would become perfect. The divine creation and the infinite existing beings would be perfected and completed, and then the Divinity of the Lord, and the names and qualities of God, on behalf of these spiritual beings, would, as regards their effect, result in laziness and inaction! "Glory to thy Lord, the Lord Who is sanctified from all their descriptions" (Qur'án 37:180).

Such were the limited minds of the former philosophers, like Ptolemy and the others who believed and imagined that the world, life and existence were restricted to this terrestrial globe, and that this boundless space was confined within the nine spheres of heaven, and that all were empty and void. Consider how greatly their thoughts were limited and how weak their minds. Those who believe in reincarnation think that the spiritual worlds are restricted to the worlds of human imagination. Moreover, some of them, like the Druzes and the Nusayris, think that existence is restricted to this physical world. What an ignorant supposition! For in this universe of God, which appears in the most complete perfection, beauty and grandeur, the luminous stars of the material universe are innumerable! Then we must reflect how limitless and infinite are the spiritual worlds, which are the essential foundation. "Take heed ye who are endued with discernment" (Qur'án 59:2).

But let us return to our subject. In the Divine Scriptures and Holy Books "return" is spoken of, but the ignorant have not understood the meaning, and those who believed in reincarnation have made conjectures on the subject. For what the divine Prophets meant by "return" is not the return of the essence, but that of the qualities; it is not the return of the Manifestation, but that of the perfections. In the Gospel it says that John, the son of Zacharias, is Elias. These words do not mean the return of the rational soul and personality of Elias in the body of John, but rather that the perfections and qualities of Elias were manifested and appeared in John.

A lamp shone in this room last night, and when tonight another lamp shines, we say the light of last night is again shining. Water flows from a fountain; then it ceases; and when it begins to flow a second time, we say, this water is the same water flowing again; or we say this light is identical with the former light. It is the same with the spring of last year, when blossoms, flowers and sweet-scented herbs bloomed, and delicious fruits were brought forth; next year we say that those delicious fruits have come back, and those blossoms, flowers and blooms have returned and come again. This does not mean that exactly the same particles composing the flowers of last year have, after decomposition, been again combined and have then come back and returned. On the contrary, the meaning is that the delicacy, freshness, delicious perfume and wonderful color of the flowers of last year are visible and apparent in exactly the same manner in the flowers of this year. Briefly, this expression refers only to the resemblance and likeness which exist between the former and latter flowers. The "return" which is mentioned in the Divine Scriptures is this: it is fully explained by the Supreme Pen [Bahá'u'lláh] in the Kitáb-i-Íqán. Refer to it, so that you may be informed of the truth of the divine mysteries.

Upon you be greetings and praise.[70]

The Five Spirits

Know that, speaking generally, there are five divisions of the spirit. First the vegetable spirit: this is a power which results from the combination of elements and the mingling of substances by the decree of the Supreme God, and from the influence, the effect and connection of other existences. When these substances and elements are separated from each other, the power of growth also ceases to exist. So, to use another figure, electricity results from the combination of elements, and when these elements are separated, the electric force is dispersed and lost. Such is the vegetable spirit.

After this is the animal spirit, which also results from the mingling and combination of elements. But this combination is more complete, and through the decree of the Almighty Lord a perfect mingling is obtained, and the animal spirit—in other words, the power of the senses—is produced. It will perceive the reality of things from that which is seen and visible, audible, edible, tangible, and that which can be smelled. After the dissociation and decomposition of the combined elements this spirit also will naturally disappear. It is like this lamp which you see: when the oil and wick and fire are brought together, light is the result; but when the oil is finished and the wick consumed, the light will also vanish and be lost.

The human spirit may be likened to the bounty of the sun shining on a mirror. The body of man, which is composed from the elements, is combined and mingled in the most perfect form; it is the most solid construction, the noblest combination, the most perfect existence. It grows and develops through the animal spirit. This perfected body can be compared to a mirror, and the human spirit to the sun. Nevertheless, if the mirror breaks, the bounty of the sun continues; and if the mirror is destroyed or ceases to exist, no harm will happen to the bounty of the sun, which is everlasting. This spirit has the power of discovery; it encompasses all things. All these wonderful signs, these scientific discoveries, great enterprises and important historical events which you know are due to it. From the realm of the invisible and hidden, through spiritual power, it brought them to the plane of the visible. So man is upon the earth, yet he makes discoveries in the heavens. From known realities—that is to say, from the things which are known and visible—he discovers unknown things. For example, man is in this hemisphere; but, like Columbus, through the power of his reason he discovers another hemisphere—that is, America—which was until then unknown. His body is heavy, but through the help of vehicles which he invents, he is able to fly. He is slow of movement, but by vehicles which he invents he travels to the East and West with extreme rapidity. Briefly, this power embraces all things.

But the spirit of man has two aspects: one divine, one satanic—that is to say, it is capable of the utmost perfection, or it is capable of the utmost imperfection. If it acquires virtues, it is the most noble of the existing beings; and if it acquires vices, it becomes the most degraded existence.

The fourth degree of spirit is the heavenly spirit; it is the spirit of faith and the bounty of God; it comes from the breath of the Holy Spirit, and by the divine power it becomes the cause of eternal life. It is the power which makes the earthly man heavenly, and the imperfect man perfect. It makes the impure to be pure, the silent eloquent; it purifies and sanctifies those made captive by carnal desires; it makes the ignorant wise.

The fifth spirit is the Holy Spirit. This Holy Spirit is the mediator between God and His creatures. It is like a mirror facing the sun. As the pure mirror receives light from the sun and transmits this bounty to others, so the Holy Spirit is the mediator of the Holy Light from the Sun of Reality, which it gives to the sanctified realities. It is adorned with all the divine perfections. Every time it appears, the world is renewed, and a new cycle is founded. The body of the world of humanity puts on a new garment. It can be compared to the spring; whenever it comes, the world passes from one condition to another. Through the advent of the season of spring the black earth and the fields and wildernesses will become verdant and blooming, and all sorts of flowers and sweet-scented herbs will grow; the trees will have new life, and new fruits will appear, and a new cycle is founded. The appearance of the Holy Spirit is like this. Whenever it appears, it renews the world of humanity and gives a new spirit to the human realities: it arrays the world of existence in a praiseworthy garment, dispels the darkness of ignorance, and causes the radiation of the light of perfections. Christ with this power has renewed this cycle; the heavenly spring with the utmost freshness and sweetness spread its tent in the world of humanity, and the life-giving breeze perfumed the nostrils of the enlightened ones.

In the same way, the appearance of Bahá'u'lláh was like a new springtime which appeared with holy breezes, with the hosts of everlasting life, and with heavenly power. It established the Throne of the Divine Kingdom in the center of the world and, by the power of the Holy Spirit, revived souls and established a new cycle.[71]

The Embryonic Formation of Man

Question: Does man in the beginning possess mind and spirit, or are they an outcome of his evolution?

Answer: The beginning of the existence of man on the terrestrial globe resembles his formation in the womb of the mother. The embryo in the womb of the mother gradually grows and develops until birth, after which it continues to grow and develop until it reaches the age of discretion and maturity. Though in infancy the signs of the mind and spirit appear in man, they do not reach the degree of perfection; they are imperfect. Only when man attains maturity do the mind and the spirit appear and become evident in utmost perfection.

So also the formation of man in the matrix of the world was in the beginning like the embryo; then gradually he made progress in perfectness, and grew and developed until he reached the state of maturity, when the mind and spirit became visible in the greatest power. In the beginning of his formation the mind and spirit also existed, but they were hidden; later they were manifested. In the womb of the world mind and spirit also existed in the embryo, but they were concealed; afterward they appeared. So it is that in the seed the tree exists, but it is hidden and concealed; when it develops and grows, the complete tree appears. In the same way the growth and development of all beings is gradual; this is the universal divine organization and the natural system. The seed does not at once become a tree; the embryo does not at once become a man; the mineral does not suddenly become a stone. No, they grow and develop gradually and attain the limit of perfection.

All beings, whether large or small, were created perfect and complete from the first, but their perfections appear in them by degrees. The organization of God is one; the evolution of existence is one; the divine system is one. Whether they be small or great beings, all are subject to one law and system. Each seed has in it from the first all the vegetable perfections. For example, in the seed all the vegetable perfections exist from the beginning, but not visibly; afterward little by little they appear. So it is first the shoot which appears from the seed, then the branches, leaves, blossoms and fruits; but from the beginning of its existence all these things are in the seed, potentially, though not apparently.

In the same way, the embryo possesses from the first all perfections, such as the spirit, the mind, the sight, the smell, the taste—in one word, all the powers—but they are not visible and become so only by degrees.

Similarly, the terrestrial globe from the beginning was created with all its elements, substances, minerals, atoms and organisms; but these only appeared by degrees: first the mineral, then the plant, afterward the animal, and finally man. But from the first these kinds and species existed, but were undeveloped in the terrestrial globe, and then appeared only gradually. For the supreme organization of God, and the universal natural system, surround all beings, and all are subject to this rule. When you consider this universal system, you see that there is not one of the beings which at its coming into existence has reached the limit of perfection. No, they gradually grow and develop, and then attain the degree of perfection.[72]

The Human Spirit Has a Beginning, But no End

Know that, although the human soul has existed on the earth for prolonged times and ages, yet it is phenomenal. As it is a divine sign, when once it has come into existence, it is eternal. The spirit of man has a beginning, but it has no end; it continues eternally. In the same way the species existing on this earth are phenomenal, for it is established that there was a time when these species did not exist on the surface of the earth. Moreover, the earth has not always existed, but the world of existence has always been, for the universe is not limited to this terrestrial globe. The meaning of this is that, although human souls are phenomenal, they are nevertheless immortal, everlasting and perpetual; for the world of things is the world of imperfection in comparison with that of man, and the world of man is the world of perfection in comparison with that of things. When imperfections reach the station of perfection, they become eternal. This is an example of which you must comprehend the meaning.[73]

The Wisdom of the Appearance of the Spirit in the Body

The wisdom of the appearance of the spirit in the body is this: the human spirit is a Divine Trust, and it must traverse all conditions, for its passage and movement through the conditions of existence will be the means of its acquiring perfections. So when a man travels and passes through different regions and numerous countries with system and method, it is certainly a means of his acquiring perfection, for he will see places, scenes and countries, from which he will discover the conditions and states of other nations. He will thus become acquainted with the geography of countries and their wonders and arts; he will familiarize himself with the habits, customs and usages of peoples; he will see the civilization and progress of the epoch; he will become aware of the policy of governments and the power and capacity of each country. It is the same when the human spirit passes through the conditions of existence: it will become the possessor of each degree and station. Even in the condition of the body it will surely acquire perfections.

Besides this, it is necessary that the signs of the perfection of the spirit should be apparent in this world, so that the world of creation may bring forth endless results, and this body may receive life and manifest the divine bounties. So, for example, the rays of the sun must shine upon the earth, and the solar heat develop the earthly beings; if the rays and heat of the sun did not shine upon the earth, the earth would be uninhabited, without meaning; and its development would be retarded. In the same way, if the perfections of the spirit did not appear in this world, this world would be unenlightened and absolutely brutal. By the appearance of the spirit in the physical form, this world is enlightened. As the spirit of man is the cause of the life of the body, so the world is in the condition of the body, and man is in the condition of the spirit. If there were no man, the perfections of the spirit would not appear, and the light of the mind would not be resplendent in this world. This world would be like a body without a soul.

This world is also in the condition of a fruit tree, and man is like the fruit; without fruit the tree would be useless.

Moreover, these members, these elements, this composition, which are found in the organism of man, are an attraction and magnet for the spirit; it is certain that the spirit will appear in it. So a mirror which is clear will certainly attract the rays of the sun. It will become luminous, and wonderful images will appear in it—that is to say, when these existing elements are gathered together according to the natural order, and with perfect strength, they become a magnet for the spirit, and the spirit will become manifest in them with all its perfections.

Under these conditions it cannot be said, "What is the necessity for the rays of the sun to descend upon the mirror?"—for the connection which exists between the reality of things, whether they be spiritual or material, requires that when the mirror is clear and faces the sun, the light of the sun must become apparent in it. In the same way, when the elements are arranged and combined in the most glorious system, organization and manner, the human spirit will appear and be manifest in them. This is the decree of the Powerful, the Wise.[74]

The Purpose of
the Soul's Journey to God

You have asked why it was necessary for the soul that was from God to make this journey back to God?...

The reality underlying this question is that the evil spirit, Satan or whatever is interpreted as evil, refers to the lower nature in man. This baser nature is symbolized in various ways. In man there are two expressions: One is the expression of nature; the other, the expression of the spiritual realm. The world of nature is defective. Look at it clearly, casting aside all superstition and imagination. If you should leave a man uneducated and barbarous in the wilds of Africa, would there be any doubt about his remaining ignorant? God has never created an evil spirit; all such ideas and nomenclature are symbols expressing the mere human or earthly nature of man. It is an essential condition of the soil of earth that thorns, weeds and fruitless trees may grow from it. Relatively speaking, this is evil; it is simply the lower state and baser product of nature.

It is evident, therefore, that man is in need of divine education and inspiration, that the spirit and bounties of God are essential to his development. That is to say, the teachings of Christ and the Prophets are necessary for his education and guidance. Why? Because They are the divine Gardeners Who till the earth of human hearts and minds. They educate man, uproot the weeds, burn the thorns and remodel the waste places into gardens and orchards where fruitful trees grow. The wisdom and purpose of Their training is that man must pass from degree to degree of progressive unfoldment until perfection is attained. For instance, if a man should live his entire life in one city, he cannot gain a knowledge of the whole world. To become perfectly informed he must visit other cities, see the mountains and valleys, cross the rivers and traverse the plains. In other words, without progressive and universal education perfection will not be attained.

Man must walk in many paths and be subjected to various processes in his evolution upward. Physically he is not born in full stature but passes through consecutive stages of fetus, infant, childhood, youth, maturity and old age. Suppose he had the power to remain young throughout his life. He then would not understand the meaning of old age and could not believe it existed. If he could not realize the condition of old age, he would not know that he was young. He would not know the difference between young and old without experiencing the old. Unless you have passed through the state of infancy, how would you know this was an infant beside you? If there were no wrong, how would you recognize the right? If it were not for sin, how would you appreciate virtue? If evil deeds were unknown, how could you commend good actions? If sickness did not exist, how would you understand health? Evil is nonexistent; it is the absence of good. Sickness is the loss of health; poverty, the lack of riches. When wealth disappears, you are poor; you look within the treasure box but find nothing there. Without knowledge there is ignorance; therefore, ignorance is simply the lack of knowledge. Death is the absence of life. Therefore, on the one hand, we have existence; on the other, nonexistence, negation or absence of existence.

Briefly, the journey of the soul is necessary. The pathway of life is the road which leads to divine knowledge and attainment. Without training and guidance the soul could never progress beyond the conditions of its lower nature, which is ignorant and defective.[75]

Human Spirit: Breath of God

Question: In the Bible it is said that God breathed the spirit into the body of man. What is the meaning of this verse?

Answer: Know that proceeding is of two kinds: the proceeding and appearance through emanation, and the proceeding and appearance through manifestation. The proceeding through emanation is like the coming forth of the action from the actor, of the writing from the writer. Now the writing emanates from the writer, and the discourse emanates from the speaker, and in the same way the human spirit emanates from God. It is not that it manifests God—that is to say, no part has been detached from the Divine Reality to enter the body of man. No, as the discourse emanates from the speaker, the spirit appears in the body of man.

But the proceeding through manifestation is the manifestation of the reality of a thing in other forms, like the coming forth of this tree from the seed of the tree, or the coming forth of the flower from the seed of the flower, for it is the seed itself which appears in the form of the branches, leaves and flowers. This is called the proceeding through manifestation. The spirits of men, with reference to God, have dependence through emanation, just as the discourse proceeds from the speaker and the writing from the writer—that is to say, the speaker himself does not become the discourse, nor does the writer himself become the writing; no, rather they have the proceeding of emanation. The speaker has perfect ability and power, and the discourse emanates from him, as the action does from the actor. The Real Speaker, the Essence of Unity, has always been in one condition, which neither changes nor alters, has neither transformation nor vicissitude. He is the Eternal, the Immortal. Therefore, the proceeding of the human spirits from God is through emanation. When it is said in the Bible that God breathed His spirit into man, this spirit is that which, like the discourse, emanates from the Real Speaker, taking effect in the reality of man.

But the proceeding through manifestation (if by this is meant the divine appearance, and not division into parts), we have said, is the proceeding and the appearance of the Holy Spirit and the Word, which is from God. As it is said in the Gospel of John, "In the beginning was the Word, and the Word was with God"; then the Holy Spirit and the Word are the appearance of God. The Spirit and the Word mean the divine perfections that appeared in the Reality of Christ, and these perfections were with God; so the sun manifests all its glory in the mirror. For the Word does not signify the body of Christ, no, but the divine perfections manifested in Him. For Christ was like a clear mirror which was facing the Sun of Reality; and the perfections of the Sun of Reality—that is to say, its light and heat—were visible and apparent in this mirror. If we look into the mirror, we see the sun, and we say, "It is the sun." Therefore, the Word and the Holy Spirit, which signify the perfections of God, are the divine appearance. This is the meaning of the verse in the Gospel which says: "The Word was with God, and the Word was God" [John 1:1]; for the divine perfections are not different from the Essence of Oneness. The perfections of

Christ are called the Word because all the beings are in the condition of letters, and one letter has not a complete meaning, while the perfections of Christ have the power of the word because a complete meaning can be inferred from a word. As the Reality of Christ was the manifestation of the divine perfections, therefore, it was like the word. Why? Because He is the sum of perfect meanings. This is why He is called the Word.

And know that the proceeding of the Word and the Holy Spirit from God, which is the proceeding and appearance of manifestation, must not be understood to mean that the Reality of Divinity had been divided into parts, or multiplied, or that it had descended from the exaltation of holiness and purity. God forbid! If a pure, fine mirror faces the sun, the light and heat, the form and the image of the sun will be resplendent in it with such manifestation that if a beholder says of the sun, which is brilliant and visible in the mirror, "This is the sun," it is true. Nevertheless, the mirror is the mirror, and the sun is the sun. The One Sun, even if it appears in numerous mirrors, is one. This state is neither abiding nor entering, neither commingling nor descending; for entering, abiding, descending, issuing forth and commingling are the necessities and characteristics of bodies, not of spirits; then how much less do they belong to the sanctified and pure Reality of God. God is exempt from all that is not in accordance with His purity and His exalted and sublime sanctity.

The Sun of Reality, as we have said, has always been in one condition; it has no change, no alteration, no transformation and no vicissitude. It is eternal and everlasting. But the Holy Reality of the Word of God is in the condition of the pure, fine and shining mirror; the heat, the light, the image and likeness—that is to say, the perfections of the Sun of Reality—appear in it. That is why Christ says in the Gospel, "The Father is in the Son"—that is to say, the Sun of Reality appears in the mirror [John 14:11; 17:21]. Praise be to the one Who shone upon this Holy Reality, Who is sanctified among the beings![76]

Relationship Between the Body, the Soul, and the Spirit

There are in the world of humanity three degrees; those of the body, the soul, and spirit.

The body is the physical or animal degree of man. From the bodily point of view man is a sharer of the animal kingdom. The bodies alike of men and animals are composed of elements held together by the law of attraction.

Like the animal, man possesses the faculties of the senses, is subject to heat, cold, hunger, thirst, etc.; unlike the animal, man has a rational soul, the human intelligence.

This intelligence of man is the intermediary between his body and his spirit.

When man allows the spirit, through his soul, to enlighten his understanding, then does he contain all Creation; because man, being the culmination of all that went before and thus superior to all previous evolutions, contains all the lower world within himself. Illumined by the spirit through the instrumentality of the soul, man's radiant intelligence makes him the crowning-point of Creation.

But on the other hand, when man does not open his mind and heart to the blessing of the spirit, but turns his soul towards the material side, towards the bodily part of his nature, then is he fallen from his high place and he becomes inferior to the inhabitants of the lower animal kingdom. In this case the man is in a sorry plight! For if the spiritual qualities of the soul, open to the breath of the Divine Spirit, are never used, they become atrophied, enfeebled, and at last incapable; whilst the soul's material qualities alone being exercised, they become terribly powerful—and the unhappy, misguided man, becomes more savage, more unjust, more vile, more cruel, more malevolent than the lower animals themselves. All his aspirations and desires being strengthened by the lower side of the soul's nature, he becomes more and more brutal, until his whole being is in no way superior to that of the beasts that perish. Men such as this, plan to work evil, to hurt and to destroy; they are entirely without the spirit of Divine compassion, for the celestial quality of the soul has been dominated by that of the material. If, on the contrary, the spiritual nature of the soul has been so strengthened that it holds the material side in subjection, then does the man approach the Divine; his humanity becomes so glorified that the virtues of the Celestial Assembly are manifested in him; he radiates the Mercy of God, he stimulates the spiritual progress of mankind, for he becomes a lamp to show light on their path.

You perceive how the soul is the intermediary between the body and the spirit. In like manner is this tree the intermediary between the seed and the fruit. When the fruit of the tree appears and becomes ripe, then we know that the tree is perfect; if the tree bore no fruit it would be merely a useless growth, serving no purpose!

When a soul has in it the life of the spirit, then does it bring forth good fruit and become a Divine tree. I wish you to try to understand this example. I hope that the unspeakable goodness of God will so strengthen you that the celestial quality of your soul, which relates it to the spirit, will for ever dominate the material side, so entirely ruling the senses that your soul will approach the perfections of the Heavenly Kingdom. May your faces, being steadfastly set towards the Divine Light, become so luminous that all your thoughts, words and actions will shine with the Spiritual Radiance dominating your souls, so that in the gatherings of the world you will show perfection in your life.

Some men's lives are solely occupied with the things of this world; their minds are so circumscribed by exterior manners and traditional interests that they are blind to any other realm of existence, to the spiritual significance of all things! They think and dream of earthly fame, of material progress. Sensuous delights and comfortable surroundings bound their horizon, their highest ambitions center in successes of worldly conditions and circumstances! They curb not their lower propensities; they eat, drink, and sleep! Like the animal, they have no thought beyond their own physical well-being. It is true that these necessities must be despatched. Life is a load which must be carried on while we are on earth, but the cares of the lower things of life should not be allowed to monopolize all the thoughts and aspirations of a human being. The heart's ambitions should ascend to a more glorious goal, mental activity should rise to higher levels! Men should hold in their souls the vision of celestial perfection, and there prepare a dwelling-place for the inexhaustible bounty of the Divine Spirit.

Let your ambition be the achievement on earth of a Heavenly civilization! I ask for you the supreme blessing, that you may be so filled with the vitality of the Heavenly Spirit that you may be the cause of life to the world.[77]

Mind, Spirit, and Soul

Question: What is the difference between the mind, spirit and soul?

Answer: ...The human spirit which distinguishes man from the animal is the rational soul, and these two names—the human spirit and the rational soul—designate one thing. This spirit, which in the terminology of the philosophers is the rational soul, embraces all beings, and as far as human ability permits discovers the realities of things and becomes cognizant of their peculiarities and effects, and of the qualities and properties of beings. But the human spirit, unless assisted by the spirit of faith, does not become acquainted with the divine secrets and the heavenly realities. It is like a mirror which, although clear, polished and brilliant, is still in need of light. Until a ray of the sun reflects upon it, it cannot discover the heavenly secrets.

But the mind is the power of the human spirit. Spirit is the lamp; mind is the light which shines from the lamp. Spirit is the tree, and the mind is the fruit. Mind is the perfection of the spirit and is its essential quality, as the sun's rays are the essential necessity of the sun.[78]

Independence of the Soul
From the Body

Paris is becoming very cold, so cold that I shall soon be obliged to go away, but the warmth of your love still keeps me here. God willing, I hope to stay among you yet a little while; bodily cold and heat cannot affect the spirit, for it is warmed by the fire of the Love of God. When we understand this, we begin to understand something of our life in the world to come.

God, in His Bounty, has given us a foretaste here, has given us certain proofs of the difference that exists between body, soul and spirit.

We see that cold, heat, suffering, etc., only concern the *body*, they do not touch the spirit.

How often do we see a man, poor, sick, miserably clad, and with no means of support, yet spiritually strong? Whatever his body has to suffer, his spirit is free and well! Again, how often do we see a rich man, physically strong and healthy, but with a soul sick unto death.

It is quite apparent to the seeing mind that a man's spirit is something very different from his physical body.

The spirit is changeless, indestructible. The progress and development of the soul, the joy and sorrow of the soul, are independent of the physical body.

If we are caused joy or pain by a friend, if a love prove true or false, it is the soul that is affected. If our dear ones are far from us—it is the soul that grieves, and the grief or trouble of the soul may react on the body.

Thus, when the spirit is fed with holy virtues, then is the body joyous; if the soul falls into sin, the body is in torment!

When we find truth, constancy, fidelity, and love, we are happy; but if we meet with lying, faithlessness, and deceit, we are miserable.

These are all things pertaining to the soul, and are not *bodily* ills. Thus, it is apparent that the soul, even as the body, has its own individuality. But if the body undergoes a change, the spirit need not be touched. When you break a glass on which the sun shines, the glass is broken, but the sun still shines! If a cage containing a bird is destroyed, the bird is unharmed! If a lamp is broken, the flame can still burn bright! The same thing applies to the spirit of man. Though death destroy his body, it has no power over his spirit—this is eternal, everlasting, both birthless and deathless.[79]

* * *

Question: After the body is put aside and the spirit has obtained freedom, in what way will the rational soul exist? Let us suppose that the souls who are assisted by the bounty of the Holy Spirit attain to true existence and eternal life. But what becomes of the rational souls—that is to say, the veiled spirits?*

Answer: Some think that the body is the substance and exists by itself, and that the spirit is accidental and depends upon the substance of the body, although, on the contrary, the rational soul is the substance, and the body depends upon it. If the accident—that is to say, the body—be destroyed, the substance, the spirit, remains.

Second, the rational soul, meaning the human spirit, does not descend into the body—that is to say, it does not enter it, for descent and entrance are characteristics of bodies, and the rational soul is exempt from this. The spirit never entered this body, so in quitting it, it will not be in need of an abiding-place: no, the spirit is connected with the body, as this light is with this mirror. When the mirror is clear and perfect, the light of the lamp will be apparent in it, and when the mirror becomes covered with dust or breaks, the light will disappear.

---

*"Veiled spirits" here signify rational souls, souls not possessing the spirit of faith.

The rational soul—that is to say, the human spirit—has neither entered this body nor existed through it; so after the disintegration of the composition of the body, how should it be in need of a substance through which it may exist? On the contrary, the rational soul is the substance through which the body exists. The personality of the rational soul is from its beginning; it is not due to the instrumentality of the body, but the state and the personality of the rational soul may be strengthened in this world; it will make progress and will attain to the degrees of perfection, or it will remain in the lowest abyss of ignorance, veiled and deprived from beholding the signs of God.[80]

Superiority of Soul Over Body

Spirit cannot be perceived by the material senses of the physical body, excepting as it is expressed in outward signs and works. The human body is visible, the soul is invisible. It is the soul nevertheless that directs a man's faculties, that governs his humanity.

The soul has two main faculties. (a) As outer circumstances are communicated to the soul by the eyes, ears, and brain of a man, so does the soul communicate its desires and purposes through the brain to the hands and tongue of the physical body, thereby expressing itself. The spirit in the soul is the very essence of life. (b) The second faculty of the soul expresses itself in the world of vision, where the soul inhabited by the spirit has its being, and functions without the help of the material bodily senses. There, in the realm of vision, the soul sees without the help of the physical eye, hears without the aid of the physical ear, and travels without dependence upon physical motion. It is, therefore, clear that the spirit in the soul of man can function through the physical body by using the organs of the ordinary senses, and that it is able also to live and act without their aid in the world of vision. This proves without a doubt the superiority of the soul of man over his body, the superiority of spirit over matter.

For example, look at this lamp: is not the light within it superior to the lamp which holds it? However beautiful the form of the lamp may be, if the light is not there its purpose is unfulfilled, it is without life—a dead thing. The lamp needs the light, but the light does not need the lamp.

The spirit does not need a body, but the body needs spirit, or it cannot live. The soul can live without a body, but the body without a soul dies.

If a man lose his sight, his hearing, his hand or his foot, should his soul still inhabit the body he lives, and is able to manifest divine virtues. On the other hand, without the spirit it would be impossible for a perfect body to exist.[81]

Mind a Radiance From the Soul

Now concerning mental faculties, they are in truth of the inherent properties of the soul, even as the radiation of light is the essential property of the sun. The rays of the sun are renewed but the sun itself is ever the same and unchanged. Consider how the human intellect develops and weakens, and may at times come to naught, whereas the soul changeth not. For the mind to manifest itself, the human body must be whole; and a sound mind cannot be but in a sound body, whereas the soul dependeth not upon the body. It is through the power of the soul that the mind comprehendeth, imagineth and exerteth its influence, whilst the soul is a power that is free. The mind comprehendeth the abstract by the aid of the concrete, but the soul hath limitless manifestations of its own. The mind is circumscribed, the soul limitless. It is by the aid of such senses as those of sight, hearing, taste, smell and touch, that the mind comprehendeth, whereas, the soul is free from all agencies. The soul as thou observest, whether it be in sleep or waking, is in motion and ever active. Possibly it may, whilst in a dream, unravel an intricate problem, incapable of solution in the waking state. The mind, moreover, understandeth not whilst the senses have ceased to function, and in the embryonic stage and in early infancy the reasoning power is totally absent, whereas the soul is ever endowed with full strength. In short, the proofs are many that go to show that despite the loss of reason, the power of the soul would still continue to exist.[82]

Soul the Inner Reality

Now regarding the question whether the faculties of the mind and the human soul are one and the same. These faculties are but the inherent properties of the soul, such as the power of imagination, of thought, of understanding; powers that are the essential requisites of the reality of man, even as the solar ray is the inherent property of the sun. The temple of man is like unto a mirror, his soul is as the sun, and his mental faculties even as the rays that emanate from that source of light. The ray may cease to fall upon the mirror, but it can in no wise be dissociated from the sun.[83]

Man Endowed With Heavenly Body

It is manifest that beyond this material body, man is endowed with another reality which is the world of exemplars constituting the heavenly body of man. In speaking, man says, "I saw," "I spoke," "I went." Who is this "I"? It is obvious that this "I" is different from this body. It is clear that when man is thinking, it is as though he were consulting with some other person. With whom is he consulting? It is evident that it is another reality or one aside from this body with whom he enters into consultation when he thinks, "Shall I do this work or not?" "What will be the result of my doing this?" Or when he questions the other reality, "What is the objection to this work if I do it?" And then that reality in man communicates its opinion to him concerning the point at issue. Therefore that reality in man is clearly and obviously other than his body, an ego with which man enters into consultation and whose opinion man seeks.

Often a man makes up his mind positively about a matter; for instance he determines to undertake a journey. Then he thinks it over, that is, he consults his inner reality and finally concludes that he will give up his journey. What has happened? Why did he abandon his original purpose? It is evident that he has consulted his inner reality which expresses to him the disadvantages of such a journey, therefore he defers to that reality and changes his original intention.

Furthermore man sees in the world of dreams. He travels in the East, he travels in the West, although his body is stationary, his body is here. It is that reality in him which makes the journey while the body sleeps. There is no doubt that a reality exists other than the outward, physical reality. Again for instance a person is dead, is buried in the ground. Afterward you see him in the world of dreams and speak with him although his body is interred in the earth. Who is the person you see in your dreams, talk to and who also speaks with you? This again proves that there is another reality different from the physical one which dies and is buried. Thus it is certain that in man there is a reality which is not the physical body. Sometimes the body becomes weak but that other reality is in its own normal state. The body goes to sleep, becomes as one dead but that reality is moving about, comprehending things, expressing them and is even conscious of itself.

This other and inner reality is called the heavenly body, the ethereal form which corresponds to this body. This is the conscious reality which discovers the inner meaning of things, for the outer body of man does not discover anything. The inner ethereal reality grasps the mysteries of existence, discovers scientific truths and indicates their technical application. It discovers electricity, produces the telegraph, the telephone and opens the door to the world of arts. If the outer material body did this, the animal would likewise be able to make scientific and wonderful discoveries, for the animal shares with man all physical powers and limitations. What then is that power which penetrates the realities of existence and which is not to be found in the animal? It is the inner reality which comprehends things, throws light upon the mysteries of life and being, discovers the heavenly Kingdom, unseals the mysteries of God and differentiates man from the brute. Of this there can be no doubt.[84]

Proofs of the Existence of Spirit

The philosophers of the world are divided into two classes: materialists, who deny the spirit and its immortality, and the divine philosophers, the wise men of God, the true illuminati who believe in the spirit and its continuance hereafter. The ancient philosophers taught that man consists simply of the material elements which compose his cellular structure and that when this composition is disintegrated the life of man becomes extinct. They reasoned that man is body only, and from this elemental composition the organs and their functions, the senses, powers and attributes which characterize man have proceeded, and that these disappear completely with the physical body. This is practically the statement of all the materialists.

The divine philosophers proclaim that the spirit of man is everliving and eternal, and because of the objections of the materialists, these wise men of God have advanced rational proofs to support the validity of their statement. Inasmuch as the materialistic philosophers deny the Books of God, Scriptural demonstration is not evidence to them, and materialistic proofs are necessary. Answering them, the men of divine knowledge have said that all existing phenomena may be resolved into grades or kingdoms, classified progressively as mineral, vegetable, animal and human, each of which possesses its degree of function and intelligence. When we consider the mineral, we find that it exists and is possessed of the power of affinity or combination. The vegetable possess the qualities of the mineral plus the augmentative virtue or power of growth. It is, therefore, evident that the vegetable kingdom is superior to the mineral. The animal kingdom in turn possesses the qualities of the mineral and vegetable plus the five senses of perception whereof the kingdoms below it are lacking. Likewise, the power of memory inherent in the animal does not exist in the lower kingdoms.

Just as the animal is more noble than the vegetable and mineral, so man is superior to the animal. The animal is bereft of ideality—that is to say, it is a captive of the world of nature and not in touch with that which lies within and beyond nature; it is without spiritual susceptibilities, deprived of the attractions of consciousness, unconscious of the world of God and incapable of deviating from the law of nature. It is different with man. Man is possessed of the emanations of consciousness; he has perception, ideality and is capable of discovering the mysteries of the universe. All the industries, inventions and facilities surrounding our daily life were at one time hidden secrets of nature, but the reality of man penetrated them and made them subject to his purposes. According to nature's laws they should have remained latent and hidden; but man, having transcended those laws, discovered these mysteries and brought them out of the plane of the invisible into the realm of the known and visible. How wonderful is the spirit of man!...

In the physical powers and senses, however, man and the animal are partners. In fact, the animal is often superior to man in sense perception. For instance, the vision of some animals is exceedingly keen and the hearing of others most acute. Consider the instinct of a dog; how much greater than that of man. But, although the animal shares with man all the physical virtues and senses, a spiritual power has been bestowed upon man of which the animal is devoid. This is a proof that there is something in man above and beyond the endowment of the animal—a faculty and virtue peculiar to the human kingdom which is lacking in the lower kingdoms of existence. This is the spirit of man. All these wonderful human accomplishments are due to the efficacy and penetrating power of the spirit of man. If man were bereft of this spirit, none of these accomplishments would have been possible. This is as evident as the sun at midday.

All the organisms of material creation are limited to an image or form. That is to say, each created material being is possessed of a form; it cannot possess two forms at the same time. For example, a body may be spherical, triangular or square; but it is impossible for it to be two of these shapes simultaneously. It may be triangular, but if it is to become square, it must first rid itself of the triangular shape. It is absolutely impossible for it to be both at the same time. Therefore, it is evident in the reality of material organisms that different forms cannot be simultaneously possessed. In the spiritual reality of man, however, all geometrical figures can be simultaneously conceived, while in physical realities one image must be forsaken in order that another may be possible. This is the law of change and transformation, and change and transformation are precursors of mortality. Were it not for this change in form, phenomena would be immortal; but because the phenomenal existence is subject to transformation, it is mortal. The reality of man, however, is possessed of all virtues; it is not necessary for him to give up one image for another as mere physical bodies do. Therefore, in that reality there is no change or transformation; it is immortal and everlasting. The body of man may be in America while his spirit is laboring and working in the Far East, discovering, organizing and planning. While occupied in governing, making laws and erecting a building in Russia, his body is still here in America. What is this power which, notwithstanding that it is embodied in America, is operating at the same time in the Orient, organizing, destroying, up-building? It is the spirit of man. This is irrefutable.

When you wish to reflect upon or consider a matter, you consult something within you. You say, shall I do it or shall I not do it? Is it better to make this journey or abandon it? Whom do you consult? Who is within you deciding this question? Surely there is a distinct power, an intelligent ego. Were it not distinct from your ego, you would not be consulting it. It is greater than the faculty of thought. It is your spirit which teaches you, which advises and decides upon matters. Who is it that interrogates? Who is it that answers? There is no doubt that it is the spirit and that there is no change or transformation in it, for it is not a composition of elements, and anything that is not composed of elements is eternal. Change and transformation are peculiarities of composition. There is no change and transformation in the spirit. In proof of this, the body may become weakened in its members. It may be dismembered, or one of its members may be incapacitated. The whole body may be paralyzed; and yet the mind, the spirit, remains ever the same. The mind decides; the thought is perfect; and yet the hand is withered, the feet have become useless, the spinal column is paralyzed, and there is no muscular movement at all, but the spirit is in the same status. Dismember a healthy man; the spirit is not dismembered. Amputate his feet; his spirit is there. He may become lame; the spirit is not affected. The spirit is ever the same; no change or transformation can you perceive, and because there is no change or trans-formation, it is everlasting and permanent.

Consider man while in the state of sleep; it is evident that all his parts and members are at a standstill, are functionless. His eye does not see, his ear does not hear, his feet and hands are motionless; but, nevertheless he does see in the world of dreams, he does hear, he speaks, he walks, he may even fly in an airplane. Therefore, it becomes evident that though the body be dead, yet the spirit is alive and permanent. Nay, the perceptions may be keener when man's body is asleep, the flight may be higher, the hearing may be more acute; all the functions are there, and yet the body is at a standstill. Hence, it is proof that there is a spirit in the man, and in this spirit there is no distinction as to whether the body be asleep or absolutely dead and dependent. The spirit is not incapacitated by these conditions; it is not bereft of its existence; it is not bereft of its perfections. The proofs are many, innumerable.

These are all rational proofs. Nobody can refute them. As we have shown that there is a spirit and that this spirit is permanent and everlasting, we must strive to learn of it. May you become informed of its power, hasten to render it divine, to have it become sanctified and holy and make it the very light of the world illumining the East and the West.[85]

The Difference Between Man And Animal

Already we have talked once or twice on the subject of the spirit, but our words have not been written down.

Know that people belong to two categories—that is to say, they constitute two parties. One party deny the spirit and say that man also is a species of animal; for they say: Do we not see that animals and men share the same powers and senses? These simple, single elements which fill space are endlessly combined, and from each of these combinations one of the beings is produced. Among these beings is the possessor of spirit, of the powers and of the senses. The more perfect the combination, the nobler is the being. The combination of the elements in the body of man is more perfect than the composition of any other being; it is mingled in absolute equilibrium; therefore, it is more noble and more perfect. "It is not," they say, "that he has a special power and spirit which the other animals lack: animals possess sensitive bodies, but man in some powers has more sensation, although, in what concerns the outer senses, such as hearing, sight, taste, smell, touch and even in some interior powers like memory, the animal is more richly endowed than man." "The animal, too," they say, "has intelligence and perception." All that they concede is that man's intelligence is greater.

This is what the philosophers of the present state; this is their saying, this is their supposition, and thus their imagination decrees. So with powerful arguments and proofs they make the descent of man go back to the animal, and say that there was once a time when man was an animal, that then the species changed and progressed little by little until it reached the present status of man.

But the theologians say: No, this is not so. Though man has powers and outer senses in common with the animal, yet an extraordinary power exists in him of which the animal is bereft. The sciences, arts, inventions, trades and discoveries of realities are the results of this spiritual power. This is a power which encompasses all things, comprehends their realities, discovers all the hidden mysteries of beings, and through this knowledge controls them. It even perceives things which do not exist outwardly—that is to say, intellectual realities which are not sensible, and which have no outward existence because they are invisible; so it comprehends the mind, the spirit, the qualities, the characters, the love and sorrow of man, which are intellectual realities. Moreover, these existing sciences, arts, laws and endless inventions of man at one time were invisible, mysterious and hidden secrets; it is only the all-encompassing human power which has discovered and brought them out from the plane of the invisible to the plane of the visible. So telegraphy, photography, phonography and all such inventions and wonderful arts were at one time hidden mysteries. The human reality discovered and brought them out from the plane of the invisible to the plane of the visible. There was even a time when the qualities of this iron which you see—indeed of all the minerals—were hidden mysteries; men discovered this mineral, and wrought it in this industrial form. It is the same with all the other discoveries and inventions of man, which are innumerable.

This we cannot deny. If we say that these are effects of powers which animals also have, and of the powers of the bodily senses, we see clearly and evidently that the animals are, in regard to these powers, superior to man. For example, the sight of animals is much more keen than the sight of man; so also is their power of smell and taste. Briefly, in the powers which animals and men have in common, the animal is often the more powerful. For example, let us take the power of memory. If you carry a pigeon from here to a distant country, and there set it free, it will return, for it remembers the way. Take a dog from here to the center of Asia, set him free, and he will come back here and never once lose the road. So it is with the other powers such as hearing, sight, smell, taste and touch.

Thus it is clear that if there were not in man a power different from any of those of the animals, the latter would be superior to man in inventions and the comprehension of realities. Therefore, it is evident that man has a gift which the animal does not possess. Now, the animal perceives sensible things but does not perceive intellectual realities. For example, that which is within the range of its vision the animal sees, but that which is beyond the range of sight it is not possible for it to perceive, and it cannot imagine it. So it is not possible for the animal to understand that the earth has the form of a globe. But man from known things proves unknown things and discovers unknown truths. For example, man sees the curve of the horizon, and from this he infers the roundness of the earth. The Pole Star at 'Akká, for instance, is at 33°—that is to say, it is 33° above the horizon. When a man goes toward the North Pole, the Pole Star rises one degree above the horizon for each degree of distance that he travels—that is to say, the altitude of the Pole Star will be 34°, then 40°, then 50°, then 60°, then 70°. If he reaches the North Pole the altitude of the Pole Star will be 90° or have attained the zenith—that is to say, will be directly over-head. This Pole Star and its ascension are sensible things. The further one goes toward the Pole, the higher the Pole Star rises; from these two known truths an unknown thing has been discovered—that is, that the horizon is curved, meaning that the horizon of each degree of the earth is a different horizon from that of another degree. Man perceives this and proves from it an invisible thing which is the roundness of the earth. This it is impossible for the animal to perceive. In the same way, it cannot understand that the sun is the center and that the earth revolves around it. The animal is the captive of the senses and bound by them; all that is beyond the senses, the things that they do not control, the animal can never understand, although in the outer senses it is greater than man. Hence it is proved and verified that in man there is a power of discovery by which he is distinguished from the animals, and this is the spirit of man.

Praise be to God! man is always turned toward the heights, and his aspiration is lofty; he always desires to reach a greater world than the world in which he is, and to mount to a higher sphere than that in which he is. The love of exaltation is one of the characteristics of man. I am astonished that certain philosophers of America and Europe are content to gradually approach the animal world and so to go backward; for the tendency of existence must be toward exaltation. Nevertheless, if you said to one of them, "You are an animal," he would be extremely hurt and angry.

What a difference between the human world and the world of the animal, between the elevation of man and the abasement of the animal, between the perfections of man and the ignorance of the animal, between the light of man and the darkness of the animal, between the glory of man and the degradation of the animal! An Arab child of ten years can manage two or three hundred camels in the desert, and with his voice can lead them forward or turn them back. A weak Hindu can so control a huge elephant that the elephant becomes the most obedient of servants. All things are subdued by the hand of man; he can resist nature while all other creatures are captives of nature: none can depart from her requirements. Man alone can resist nature. Nature attracts bodies to the center of the earth; man through mechanical means goes far from it and soars in the air. Nature prevents man from crossing the seas; man builds a ship, and he travels and voyages across the great ocean, and so on; the subject is endless. For example, man drives engines over the mountains and through the wildernesses, and gathers in one spot the news of the events of the East and West. All this is contrary to nature. The sea with its grandeur cannot deviate by an atom from the laws of nature; the sun in all its magnificence cannot deviate as much as a needle's point from the laws of nature, and can never comprehend the conditions, the state, the qualities, the movements and the nature of man.

What, then, is the power in this small body of man which encompasses all this? What is this ruling power by which he subdues all things?

One more point remains. Modern philosophers say: "We have never seen the spirit in man, and in spite of our researches into the secrets of the human body, we do not perceive a spiritual power. How can we imagine a power which is not sensible?" The theologians reply: "The spirit of the animal also is not sensible, and through its bodily powers it cannot be perceived. By what do you prove the existence of the spirit of the animal? There is no doubt that from its effects you prove that in the animal there is a power which is not in the plant, and this is the power of the senses—that is to say, sight, hearing and also other powers; from these you infer that there is an animal spirit. In the same way, from the proofs and signs we have mentioned, we argue that there is a human spirit. Since in the animal there are signs which are not in the plant, you say this power of sensation is a property of the animal spirit; you also see in man signs, powers and perfections which do not exist in the animal; therefore, you infer that there is a power in him which the animal is without."

If we wish to deny everything that is not sensible, then we must deny the realities which unquestionably exist. For example, ethereal matter is not sensible, though it has an undoubted existence. The power of attraction is not sensible, though it certainly exists. From what do we affirm these existences? From their signs. Thus this light is the vibration of that ethereal matter, and from this vibration we infer the existence of ether.[86]

Animals Without Soul

When asked about the individual persistence of the animal's personality after death, 'Abdu'l-Bahá said: "Even the most developed dog has not the immortal soul of the man; yet the dog is perfect in its own place. You do not quarrel with a rose-tree because it cannot sing!"[87]

Immortality of the Spirit (I)

The whole physical creation is perishable. These material bodies are composed of atoms; when these atoms begin to separate decomposition sets in, then comes what we call death. This composition of atoms, which constitutes the body or mortal element of any created being, is temporary. When the power of attraction, which holds these atoms together, is withdrawn, the body, as such, ceases to exist.

With the soul it is different. The soul is not a combination of elements, it is not composed of many atoms, it is of one indivisible substance and therefore eternal. It is entirely out of the order of the physical creation; it is immortal!

Scientific philosophy has demonstrated that a *simple* element ('simple' meaning 'not composed') is indestructible, eternal. The soul, not being a composition of elements, is, in character, as a simple element, and therefore cannot cease to exist.

The soul, being of that one indivisible substance, can suffer neither disintegration nor destruction, therefore there is no reason for its coming to an end. All things living show signs of their existence, and it follows that these signs could not of themselves exist if that which they express or to which they testify had no being. A thing which does not exist, can, of course, give no sign of its existence. The manifold signs of the existence of the spirit are for ever before us.

The traces of the Spirit of Jesus Christ, the influence of His Divine Teaching, is present with us today, and is everlasting.

A non-existent thing, it is agreed, cannot be seen by signs. In order to write, a man must exist—one who does not exist cannot write. Writing is, in itself, a sign of the writer's soul and intelligence. The Sacred Writings (with ever the same Teaching) prove the continuity of the spirit.

Consider the aim of creation: is it possible that all is created to evolve and develop through countless ages with this small goal in view—a few years of a man's life on earth? Is it not unthinkable that this should be the final aim of existence?

The mineral evolves till it is absorbed in the life of the plant, the plant progresses till finally it loses its life in that of the animal; the animal, in its turn, forming part of the food of man, is absorbed into human life.

Thus, man is shown to be the sum of all creation, the superior of all created beings, the goal to which countless ages of existence have progressed.

At the best, man spends four-score years and ten in this world—a short time indeed!

Does a man cease to exist when he leaves the body? If his life comes to an end, then all the previous evolution is useless, all has been for nothing! Can one imagine that Creation has no greater aim than this?

The soul is eternal, immortal.

Materialists say, 'Where is the soul? What is it? We cannot see it, neither can we touch it.'

This is how we must answer them: However much the mineral may progress, it cannot comprehend the vegetable world. Now, that lack of comprehension does not prove the non-existence of the plant!

To however great a degree the plant may have evolved, it is unable to understand the animal world; this ignorance is no proof that the animal does not exist!

The animal...cannot imagine the intelligence of man, neither can he realize the nature of his soul. But, again, this does not prove that man is without intellect, or without soul. It only demonstrates this, that one form of existence is incapable of comprehending a form superior to itself

This flower may be unconscious of such a being as man, but the fact of its ignorance does not prevent the existence of humanity.

In the same way, if materialists do not believe in the existence of the soul, their unbelief does not prove that there is no such realm as the world of spirit. The very existence of man's intelligence proves his immortality; moreover, darkness proves the presence of light, for without light there would be no shadow. Poverty proves the existence of riches, for, without riches, how could we measure poverty? Ignorance proves that knowledge exists, for without knowledge how could there be ignorance?

Therefore the idea of mortality presupposes the existence of immortality—for if there were no Life Eternal, there would be no way of measuring the life of this world!

If the spirit were not immortal, how could the Manifestations of God endure such terrible trials?

Why did Christ Jesus suffer the fearful death on the cross?

Why did Muhammad bear persecutions?

Why did the Báb make the supreme sacrifice and why did Bahá'u'lláh pass the years of his life in prison?

Why should all this suffering have been, if not to prove the everlasting life of the spirit?

Christ suffered, He accepted all His trials because of the immortality of His spirit. If a man reflects he will understand the spiritual significance of the law of progress; how all moves from the inferior to the superior degree.

It is only a man without intelligence who, after considering these things, can imagine that the great scheme of creation should suddenly cease to progress, that evolution should come to such an inadequate end!

Materialists who reason in this way, and contend that we are unable to *see* the world of spirit, or to perceive the blessings of God, are surely like the animals who have no understanding; having eyes they see not, ears they have, but do not hear. And this lack of sight and hearing is a proof of nothing but their own inferiority; of whom we read in the Qur'án, 'They are men who are blind and deaf to the Spirit.' They do not use that great gift of God, the power of the understanding, by which they might see with the eyes of the spirit, hear with spiritual ears and also comprehend with a Divinely enlightened heart.

The inability of the materialistic mind to grasp the idea of the Life Eternal is no proof of the non-existence of that life.

The comprehension of that other life depends on our spiritual birth!

My prayer for you is that your spiritual faculties and aspirations may daily increase, and that you will never allow the material senses to veil from your eyes the glories of the Heavenly Illumination.[88]

Immortality of the Spirit (II)

The logical proof of the immortality of the spirit is this, that no sign can come from a nonexisting thing—that is to say, it is impossible that from absolute nonexistence signs should appear—for the signs are the consequence of an existence, and the consequence depends upon the existence of the principle. So from a nonexisting sun no light can radiate; from a nonexisting sea no waves appear; from a nonexisting cloud no rain falls; a nonexisting tree yields no fruit; a nonexisting man neither manifests nor produces anything. Therefore, as long as signs of existence appear, they are a proof that the possessor of the sign is existent.

Consider that today the Kingdom of Christ exists. From a nonexisting king how could such a great kingdom be manifested? How, from a nonexisting sea, can the waves mount so high? From a nonexisting garden, how can such fragrant breezes be wafted? Reflect that no effect, no trace, no influence remains of any being after its members are dispersed and its elements are decomposed, whether it be a mineral, a vegetable or an animal. There is only the human reality and the spirit of man which, after the disintegration of the members, dispersing of the particles, and the destruction of the composition, persists and continues to act and to have power.

This question is extremely subtle: consider it attentively. This is a rational proof which we are giving, so that the wise may weigh it in the balance of reason and justice. But if the human spirit will rejoice and be attracted to the Kingdom of God, if the inner sight becomes opened, and the spiritual hearing strengthened, and the spiritual feelings predominant, he will see the immortality of the spirit as clearly as he sees the sun, and the glad tidings and signs of God will encompass him.[89]

Immortality of the Spirit (III)

Know that the power and the comprehension of the human spirit are of two kinds—that is to say, they perceive and act in two different modes. One way is through instruments and organs: thus with this eye it sees; with this ear it hears; with this tongue it talks. Such is the action of the spirit, and the perception of the reality of man, by means of organs— that is to say, that the spirit is the seer, through the eyes; the spirit is the hearer, through the ear; the spirit is the speaker, through the tongue.

The other manifestation of the powers and actions of the spirit is without instruments and organs. For example, in the state of sleep without eyes it sees; without an ear it hears; without a tongue it speaks; without feet it runs. Briefly, these actions are beyond the means of instruments and organs. How often it happens that it sees a dream in the world of sleep, and its signification becomes apparent two years afterward in corresponding events. In the same way, how many times it happens that a question which one cannot solve in the world of wakefulness is solved in the world of dreams. In wakefulness the eye sees only for a short distance, but in dreams he who is in the East sees the West. Awake he sees the present; in sleep he sees the future. In wakefulness, by means of rapid transit, at the most he can travel only twenty farsakhs* an hour; in sleep, in the twinkling of an eye, he traverses the East and West. For the spirit travels in two different ways: without means, which is spiritual traveling; and with means, which is material traveling: as birds which fly, and those which are carried.

In the time of sleep this body is as though dead; it does not see nor hear; it does not feel; it has no consciousness, no perception—that is to say, the powers of man have become inactive, but the spirit lives and subsists. Nay, its penetration is increased, its flight is higher, and its intelligence is greater.

To consider that after the death of the body the spirit perishes is like imagining that a bird in a cage will be destroyed if the cage is broken, though the bird has nothing to fear from the destruction of the cage. Our body is like the cage, and the spirit is like the bird. We see that without the cage this bird flies in the world of sleep; therefore, if the cage becomes broken, the bird will continue and exist. Its feelings will be even more powerful, its perceptions greater, and its happiness increased. In truth, from hell it reaches a paradise of delights because for the thankful birds there is no paradise greater than freedom from the cage. That is why with utmost joy and happiness the martyrs hasten to the plain of sacrifice.

In wakefulness the eye of man sees at the utmost as far as one hour of distance* because through the instrumentality of the body the power of the spirit is thus determined; but with the inner sight and the mental eye it sees America, and it can perceive that which is there, and discover the conditions

---

*One farsakh is equivalent to about four miles.

*It is a Persian custom to reckon distance by time.

of things and organize affairs. If, then, the spirit were the same as the body, it would be necessary that the power of the inner sight should also be in the same proportion. Therefore, it is evident that this spirit is different from the body, and that the bird is different from the cage, and that the power and penetration of the spirit is stronger without the intermediary of the body. Now, if the instrument is abandoned, the possessor of the instrument continues to act. For example, if the pen is abandoned or broken, the writer remains living and present; if a house is ruined, the owner is alive and existing. This is one of the logical evidences for the immortality of the soul.

There is another: this body becomes weak or heavy or sick, or it finds health; it becomes tired or rested; sometimes the hand or leg is amputated, or its physical power is crippled; it becomes blind or deaf or dumb; its limbs may become paralyzed; briefly, the body may have all the imperfections. Nevertheless, the spirit in its original state, in its own spiritual perception, will be eternal and perpetual; it neither finds any imperfection, nor will it become crippled. But when the body is wholly subjected to disease and misfortune, it is deprived of the bounty of the spirit, like a mirror which, when it becomes broken or dirty or dusty, cannot reflect the rays of the sun nor any longer show its bounties.

We have already explained that the spirit of man is not in the body because it is freed and sanctified from entrance and exit, which are bodily conditions. The concoction of the spirit with the body is like that of the sun with the mirror. Briefly, the human spirit is in one condition. It neither becomes ill from the diseases of the body nor cured by its health; it does not become sick, nor weak, nor miserable, nor poor, nor light, nor small—that is to say, it will not be injured because of the infirmities of the body, and no effect will be visible even if the body becomes weak, or if the hands and feet and tongue be cut off, or if it loses the power of hearing or sight. Therefore, it is evident and certain that the spirit is different from the body, and that its duration is independent of that of the body; on the contrary, the spirit with the utmost greatness rules in the world of the body; and its power and influence, like the bounty of the sun in the mirror, are apparent and visible. But when the mirror becomes dusty or breaks, it will cease to reflect the rays of the sun.[90]

The Perishable And Imperishable

The earthly things have an existence, though they must perish. All creatures have this same existence; all created things must die. The wise man sees them as perished. But that which belongs to the Divine Kingdom of Heaven is everlasting. The souls of those who are awake and mindful will take heed unto this and turn to the Everlasting Kingdom before it is too late. The outward and perishable is but the sign of the inward and imperishable. How many celebrated people have come and gone since Christ lived! How many kings and princes, famous men, and men considered wonderful for their learning have arisen and passed away! No sign of them remains, no result, therefore no existence. But those humble, meek, and unimportant men who partook of the Cup of Christ's Teachings shine forever in the Spiritual Horizon, although they were looked upon as having no knowledge. That which is of the Divine Kingdom is everlasting; that which belongs to the kingdom of the world will fade away and perish.[91]

Human Life Cannot End Here

All divine philosophers and men of wisdom and understanding, when observing these endless beings, have considered that in this great and infinite universe all things end in the mineral kingdom, that the outcome of the mineral kingdom is the vegetable kingdom, the outcome of the vegetable kingdom is the animal kingdom and the outcome of the animal kingdom the world of man. The consummation of this limitless universe with all its grandeur and glory hath been man himself, who in this world of being toileth and suffereth for a time, with diverse ills and pains, and ultimately disintegrates, leaving no trace and no fruit after him. Were it so, there is no doubt that this infinite universe with all its perfections has ended in shame and delusion with no result, no fruit, no permanence and no effect. It would be utterly without meaning. They were thus convinced that such is not the case, that this Great Workshop with all its power, its bewildering magnificence and endless perfections, cannot eventually come to naught. That still another life should exist is thus certain, and, just as the vegetable kingdom is unaware of the world of man, so we, too, know not of the Great Life hereafter that followeth the life of man here below. Our non-comprehension of that life, however, is no proof of its non-existence. The mineral world, for instance, is utterly unaware of the world of man and cannot comprehend it, but the ignorance of a thing is no proof of its nonexistence. Numerous and conclusive proofs exist that go to show that this infinite world cannot end with this human life.[92]

Planning For the Future

The wise man works not for the present moment but for the good results of the future. See in the winter how bare and lifeless the trees and plants seem, without leaves and without fruit. Suppose one should pass by at this time who knew nothing of the condition of the earth and saw a man ploughing it up and casting grain in the furrow. Would he not say, "How foolish this man is. He is troubling himself for no result, working for no purpose and wasting that which would give him food?" But in due time the showers descend upon the earth, the sun shines, the breezes blow and we see the result in a great beauty and production.[93]

Looking Forward to Death

A friend asked: "How should one look forward to death?"

'Abdu'l-Bahá answered: "How does one look forward to the goal of any journey? With hope and with expectation. It is even so with the end of this earthly journey. In the next world, man will find himself freed from many of the disabilities under which he now suffers. Those who have passed on through death, have a sphere of their own. It is not removed from ours; their work, the work of the Kingdom, is ours; but it is sanctified from what we call 'time and place.' Time with us is measured by the sun. When there is no more sunrise, and no more sunset, that kind of time does not exist for man. Those who have ascended have different attributes from those who are still on earth, yet there is no real separation."[94]

The Imperishable Gift

O thou who art attracted to the Kingdom of God! Every soul seeketh an object and cherisheth a desire, and day and night striveth to attain his aim. One craveth riches, another thirsteth for glory and still another yearneth for fame, for art, for prosperity and the like. Yet finally all are doomed to loss and disappointment. One and all they leave behind them all that is theirs and empty-handed hasten to the realm beyond, and all their labors shall be in vain. To dust they shall all return, denuded, depressed, disheartened and in utter despair.

But, praised be the Lord, thou art engaged in that which secureth for thee a gain that shall eternally endure; and that is naught but thine attraction to the Kingdom of God, thy faith, and thy knowledge, the enlightenment of thine heart, and thine earnest endeavor to promote the Divine Teachings.

Verily this gift is imperishable and this wealth is a treasure from on high![95]

The Eternal Beauty of God

Mortal charm shall fade away, roses shall give way to thorns, and beauty and youth shall live their day and be no more. But that which eternally endureth is the Beauty of the True One, for its splendor perisheth not and its glory lasteth for ever; its charm is all-powerful and its attraction infinite. Well is it then with that countenance that reflecteth the splendor of the Light of the Beloved One! The Lord be praised, thou hast been illumined with this Light, hast acquired the pearl of true knowledge, and hast spoken the Word of Truth.[96]

This Mortal Life

This phenomenal world will not remain in an unchanging condition even for a short while. Second after second it undergoes change and transformation. Every foundation will finally become collapsed; every glory and splendor will at last vanish and disappear, but the Kingdom of God is eternal and the heavenly sovereignty and majesty will stand firm, everlasting. Hence in the estimation of a wise man the mat in the Kingdom of God is preferable to the throne of the government of the world.[97]

This Life a Drifting Shadow

O thou handmaid aflame with the fire of God's love! Grieve thou not over the troubles and hardships of this nether world, nor be thou glad in times of ease and comfort, for both shall pass away. This present life is even as a swelling wave, or a mirage, or drifting shadows. Could ever a distorted image on the desert serve as refreshing waters? No, by the Lord of Lords! Never can reality and the mere semblance of reality be one, and wide is the difference between fancy and fact, between truth and the phantom thereof.

Know thou that the Kingdom is the real world, and this nether place is only its shadow stretching out. A shadow hath no life of its own; its existence is only a fantasy, and nothing more; it is but images reflected in water, and seeming as pictures to the eye.[98]

Next Life the Fruit of This Life

When thou lookest about thee with a perceptive eye, thou wilt note that on this dusty earth all humankind are suffering. Here is no man at rest, to compensate for sins he expiated in a former life; nor is there anyone so blissful as seemingly to pluck the fruit of bygone anguish. And if a human life, with its spiritual being, were limited to this earthly span, then what would be the harvest of creation? Indeed, what would be the effects and the outcomes of Divinity Itself? Were such a notion true, then all created things, all contingent realities, and this whole world of being—all would be meaningless. God forbid that one should hold to such a fiction and gross error.

For just as the effects and the fruitage of the uterine life are not to be found in that dark and narrow place, and only when the child is transferred to this wide earth do the benefits and uses of growth and development in that previous world become revealed—so likewise reward and punishment, heaven and hell, requital and retribution for actions done in this present life, will stand revealed in that other world beyond. And just as, if human life in the womb were limited to that uterine world, existence there would be nonsensical, irrelevant—so too if the life of this world, the deeds here done and their fruitage, did not come forth in the world beyond, the whole process would be irrational and foolish.

Know then that the Lord God possesseth invisible realms which the human intellect can never hope to fathom nor the mind of man conceive. When once thou hast cleansed the channel of thy spiritual sense from the pollution of this worldly life, then wilt thou breathe in the sweet scents of holiness that blow from the blissful bowers of that heavenly land.[99]

A Desire to Return For Service

The souls of the well-favored among the concourse on high, the sacred dwellers of the most exalted Paradise, are in this day filled with burning desire to return unto this world, that they may render such service as lieth in their power to the threshold of the Abhá Beauty [Bahá'u'lláh].[100]

This World a Mirage

O ye loved ones of God! Know ye that the world is even as a mirage rising over the sands, that the thirsty mistaketh for water. The wine of this world is but a vapor in the desert, its pity and compassion but toil and trouble, the repose it proffereth only weariness and sorrow. Abandon it to those who belong to it, and turn your faces unto the Kingdom of your Lord the All-Merciful, that His grace and bounty may cast their dawning splendors over you, and a heavenly table may be sent down for you, and your Lord may bless you, and shower His riches upon you to gladden your bosoms and fill your hearts with bliss, to attract your minds, and cleanse your souls, and console your eyes.[101]

Perfect Happiness in the Kingdom

All the sufferings you pass through in gaining the Kingdom of God will be obliterated when you attain its perfect happiness. It is as a man who has been ill and helpless for two or three years and afterwards becomes well and strong, then all remembrance of his pain vanishes. The happiness of the Kingdom is a perfect one unlike the imperfection of our best earthly conditions and is never again to be clouded by any vestige of sorrow. Whatever troubles we have on our way to the Kingdom are a test to the soul. When man enters this world it is in troubles and hardships, but he comes from the invisible to the visible to gain great things for himself. As the material birth is a time of trouble, so also is the spiritual. The way to God is strewn with troubles and difficulties, but remember always what Christ said: "Though the body is weak the spirit is powerful."[102]

Seeking the Glory of Heaven

These few brief days shall pass away, this present life shall vanish from our sight; the roses of this world shall be fresh and fair no more, the garden of this earth's triumphs and delights shall droop and fade. The spring season of life shall turn into the autumn of death, the bright joy of palace shall give way to moonless dark within the tomb. And therefore is none of this worth loving at all, and to this the wise will not anchor his heart.

He who hath knowledge and power will rather seek out the glory of heaven, and spiritual distinction, and the life that dieth not. And such a one longeth to approach the sacred Threshold of God; for in the tavern of this swiftly-passing world the man of God will not lie drunken, nor will he even for a moment take his ease, nor stain himself with any fondness for this earthly life.[103]

Part IV

Prayers

A Special Prayer for the Departed*

O my God! This is Thy servant and the son of Thy servant who hath believed in Thee and in Thy signs, and set his face towards Thee, wholly detached from all except Thee. Thou art, verily, of those who show mercy the most merciful.

Deal with him, O Thou Who forgivest the sins of men and concealest their faults, as beseemeth the heaven of Thy bounty and the ocean of Thy grace. Grant him admission within the precincts of Thy transcendent mercy that was before the foundation of earth and heaven. There is no God but Thee, the Ever-Forgiving, the Most Generous.

> Let him, then, repeat six times the greeting "Alláh-u-Abhá," and then repeat nineteen times each of the following verses:

We all, verily, worship God.

We all, verily, bow down before God.

We all, verily, are devoted unto God.

We all, verily, give praise unto God.

We all, verily, yield thanks unto God.

We all, verily, are patient in God.

> (If the dead be a woman, let him say: This is Thy handmaiden and the daughter of Thy handmaiden, etc.)[1]
> Bahá'u'lláh

---

*The Prayer for the Dead is to be used for Bahá'ís over the age of fifteen. "It is the only Bahá'í obligatory prayer which is to be recited in congregation; it is to be recited by one believer while all present stand. There is no requirement to face the Shrine of Bahá'u'lláh when reciting this prayer."[2]

On the finger of the departed should be placed a ring on which this prayer is inscribed: "I came forth from God, and return unto Him, detached from all save Him, holding fast to His Name, the Merciful, the Compassionate."[3]

Prayers for the Departed

Glory be to Thee, O Lord my God! Abase not him whom Thou hast exalted through the power of Thine everlasting sovereignty, and remove not far from Thee him whom Thou hast caused to enter the tabernacle of Thine eternity. Wilt Thou cast away, O my God, him whom Thou hast overshadowed with Thy Lordship, and wilt Thou turn away from Thee, O my Desire, him to whom Thou hast been a refuge? Canst Thou degrade him whom Thou hast uplifted, or forget him whom Thou didst enable to remember Thee?

Glorified, immensely glorified art Thou! Thou art He Who from everlasting hath been the King of the entire creation and its Prime Mover, and Thou wilt to everlasting remain the Lord of all created things and their Ordainer. Glorified art Thou, O my God! If Thou ceasest to be merciful unto Thy servants, who, then, will show mercy unto them; and if Thou refusest to succor Thy loved ones, who is there that can succor them?

Glorified, immeasurably glorified art Thou! Thou art adored in Thy truth, and Thee do we all, verily, worship; and Thou art manifest in Thy justice, and to Thee do we all, verily, bear witness. Thou art, in truth, beloved in Thy grace. No God is there but Thee, the Help in Peril, the Self-Subsisting.[4]   Bahá'u'lláh

* * *

Say: O God, my God! Thou hast committed into mine hands a trust from Thee, and hast now according to the good-pleasure of Thy Will called it back to Thyself. It is not for me, who am a handmaid of Thine, to say...wherefore hath it happened, inasmuch as Thou art glorified in all Thine acts, and art to be obeyed in Thy decree.

Thine handmaid, O my Lord, hath set her hopes on Thy grace and bounty. Grant that she may obtain that which will draw her nigh unto Thee, and will profit her in every world of Thine. Thou art the Forgiving, the All-Bountiful. There is none other God but Thee, the Ordainer, the Ancient of Days.[5]

Bahá'u'lláh

* * *

He is God, exalted is He, the Lord of loving-kindness and bounty!

Glory be unto Thee, Thou, O my God, the Lord Omnipotent. I testify to Thine omnipotence and Thy might, Thy sovereignty and Thy loving-kindness, Thy grace and Thy power, the oneness of Thy Being and the unity of Thine Essence, Thy sanctity and exaltation above the world of being and all that is therein.

O my God! Thou seest me detached from all save Thee, holding fast unto Thee and turning unto the ocean of Thy bounty, to the heaven of Thy favor, to the Daystar of Thy grace.

Lord! I bear witness that in Thy servant Thou hast reposed Thy Trust, and that is the Spirit wherewith Thou hast given life to the world.

I ask of Thee by the splendor of the Orb of Thy Revelation, mercifully to accept from him that which he hath achieved in Thy days. Grant then that he may be invested with the glory of Thy good-pleasure and adorned with Thine acceptance.

O my Lord! I myself and all created things bear witness unto Thy might, and I pray Thee not to turn away from Thyself this spirit that hath ascended unto Thee, unto Thy heavenly place, Thine exalted Paradise and Thy retreats of nearness, O Thou who art the Lord of all men!

Grant, then, O my God, that Thy servant may consort with Thy chosen ones, Thy saints and Thy Messengers in heavenly places that the pen cannot tell nor the tongue recount.

O My Lord, the poor one hath verily hastened unto the Kingdom of Thy wealth, the stranger unto his home within Thy precincts, he that is sore athirst to the heavenly river of Thy bounty. Deprive him not, O Lord, from his share of the banquet of Thy grace and from the favor of Thy bounty. Thou art in truth the Almighty, the Gracious, the All-Bountiful.

O my God, Thy Trust hath been returned unto Thee. It behooveth Thy grace and Thy bounty that have compassed Thy dominions on earth and in heaven, to vouchsafe unto Thy newly welcomed one Thy gifts and Thy bestowals, and the fruits of the tree of Thy grace! Powerful art Thou to do as Thou willest, there is none other God but Thee, the Gracious, the Most Bountiful, the Compassionate, the Bestower, the Pardoner, the Precious, the All-Knowing.

I testify, O my Lord, that Thou hast enjoined upon men to honor their guest, and he that hath ascended unto Thee hath verily reached Thee and attained Thy Presence. Deal with him then according to Thy grace and bounty! By Thy glory, I know of a certainty that Thou wilt not withhold Thyself from that which Thou hast commanded Thy servants, nor wilt Thou deprive him that hath clung to the cord of Thy bounty and hath ascended to the Dayspring of Thy wealth.

There is none other God but Thee, the One, the Single, the Powerful, the Omniscient, the Bountiful.[6]   Bahá'u'lláh

* * *

Lauded art Thou, O my God, my trespasses have waxed mighty and my sins have assumed grievous proportions. How disgraceful my plight will prove to be in Thy holy presence. I have failed to know Thee to the extent Thou didst reveal Thyself unto me; I have failed to worship Thee with a devotion worthy of Thy summons; I have failed to obey Thee through not treading the path of Thy love in the manner Thou didst inspire me.

Thy might beareth me witness, O my God, what befitteth Thee is far greater and more exalted than any being could attempt to accomplish. Indeed nothing can ever comprehend Thee as is worthy of Thee nor can any servile creature worship Thee as beseemeth Thine adoration. So perfect and comprehensive is Thy proof, O my God, that its inner essence transcendeth the description of any soul and so abundant are the outpourings of Thy gifts that no faculty can appraise their infinite range.

O my God! O my Master! I beseech Thee by Thy manifold bounties and by the pillars which sustain Thy throne of glory, to have pity on these lowly people who are powerless to bear the unpleasant things of this fleeting life, how much less then can they bear Thy chastisement in the life to come—a chastisement which is ordained by Thy justice, called forth by Thy wrath and will continue to exist for ever.

I beg Thee by Thyself, O my God, my Lord and my Master, to intercede in my behalf. I have fled from Thy justice unto Thy mercy. For my refuge I am seeking Thee and such as turn not away from Thy path, even for a twinkling of an eye—they for whose sake Thou didst create the creation as a token of Thy grace and bounty.[7]   The Báb

* * *

Praise be unto Thee, O Lord. Forgive us our sins, have mercy upon us and enable us to return unto Thee. Suffer us not to rely on aught else besides Thee, and vouchsafe unto us, through Thy bounty, that which Thou lovest and desirest and well beseemeth Thee. Exalt the station of them that have truly believed and forgive them with Thy gracious forgiveness. Verily Thou art the Help in Peril, the Self-Subsisting.[8]   The Báb

* * *

I beg Thy forgiveness, O my God, and implore pardon after the manner Thou wishest Thy servants to direct themselves to Thee. I beg of Thee to wash away our sins as befitteth Thy Lordship, and to forgive me, my parents, and those who in Thy estimation have entered the abode of Thy love in a manner which is worthy of Thy transcendent sovereignty and well beseemeth the glory of Thy celestial power.

O my God! Thou hast inspired my soul to offer its supplication to Thee, and but for Thee, I would not call upon Thee. Lauded and glorified art Thou; I yield Thee praise inasmuch as Thou didst reveal Thyself unto me, and I beg Thee to forgive me, since I have fallen short in my duty to know Thee and have failed to walk in the path of Thy love.[9]

The Báb

* * *

I am aware, O Lord, that my trespasses have covered my face with shame in Thy presence, and have burdened my back before Thee, have intervened between me and Thy beauteous countenance, have compassed me from every direction and have hindered me on all sides from gaining access unto the revelations of Thy celestial power.

O Lord! If Thou forgivest me not, who is there then to grant pardon, and if Thou hast no mercy upon me who is capable of showing compassion? Glory be unto Thee, Thou didst create me when I was non-existent and Thou didst nourish me while I was devoid of any understanding. Praise be unto Thee, every evidence of bounty proceedeth from Thee and every token of grace emanateth from the treasuries of Thy decree.[10]   The Báb

* * *

O God our Lord! Protect us through Thy grace from whatsoever may be repugnant unto Thee and vouchsafe unto us that which well beseemeth Thee. Give us more out of Thy bounty and bless us. Pardon us for the things we have done and wash away our sins and forgive us with Thy gracious forgiveness. Verily Thou art the Most Exalted, the Self-Subsisting.

Thy loving providence hath encompassed all created things in the heavens and on the earth, and Thy forgiveness hath surpassed the whole creation. Thine is sovereignty; in Thy hand are the Kingdoms of Creation and Revelation; in Thy right hand Thou holdest all created things and within Thy grasp are the assigned measures of forgiveness. Thou forgivest whomsoever among Thy servants Thou pleasest. Verily Thou art the Ever-Forgiving, the All-Loving. Nothing whatsoever escapeth Thy knowledge, and naught is there which is hidden from Thee.

O God our Lord! Protect us through the potency of Thy might, enable us to enter Thy wondrous surging ocean, and grant us that which well befitteth Thee.

Thou art the Sovereign Ruler, the Mighty Doer, the Exalted, the All-Loving.[11]   The Báb

* * *

Glory be unto Thee, O God. How can I make mention of Thee while Thou art sanctified from the praise of all mankind. Magnified be Thy Name, O God, Thou art the King, the Eternal Truth; Thou knowest what is in the heavens and on the earth, and unto Thee must all return. Thou hast sent down Thy divinely-ordained Revelation according to a clear measure. Praised art Thou, O Lord! At Thy behest Thou dost render victorious whomsoever Thou willest, through the hosts of heaven and earth and whatsoever existeth between them. Thou art the Sovereign, the Eternal Truth, the Lord of invincible might.

Glorified art Thou, O Lord, Thou forgivest at all times the sins of such among Thy servants as implore Thy pardon. Wash away my sins and the sins of those who seek Thy forgiveness at dawn, who pray to Thee in the day-time and in the night season, who yearn after naught save God, who offer up whatsoever God hath graciously bestowed upon them, who celebrate Thy praise at morn and eventide, and who are not remiss in their duties.[12]   The Báb

* * *

O my God! O Thou forgiver of sins, bestower of gifts, dispeller of afflictions!

Verily, I beseech Thee to forgive the sins of such as have abandoned the physical garment and have ascended to the spiritual world.

O my Lord! Purify them from trespasses, dispel their sorrows, and change their darkness into light. Cause them to enter the garden of happiness, cleanse them with the most pure water, and grant them to behold Thy splendors on the loftiest mount.[13]   'Abdu'l-Bahá

* * *

O my God! O my God! Verily, Thy servant, humble before the majesty of Thy divine supremacy, lowly at the door of Thy oneness, hath believed in Thee and in Thy verses, hath testified to Thy word, hath been enkindled with the fire of Thy love, hath been immersed in the depths of the ocean of Thy knowledge, hath been attracted by Thy breezes, hath relied upon Thee, hath turned his face to Thee, hath offered his supplications to Thee, and hath been assured of Thy pardon and forgiveness. He hath abandoned this mortal life and hath flown to the kingdom of immortality, yearning for the favor of meeting Thee.

O Lord, glorify his station, shelter him under the pavilion of Thy supreme mercy, cause him to enter Thy glorious paradise, and perpetuate his existence in Thine exalted rose garden, that he may plunge into the sea of light in the world of mysteries.

Verily, Thou art the Generous, the Powerful, the Forgiver and the Bestower.[14]   'Abdu'l-Bahá

Part V

Selections From the Qur'án

This section offers quotations from the Qur'án. It is divided into five parts. The first part presents a cross-section of the Qur'ánic teachings on the afterlife, the others offer references on specific topics. As you read this section, keep in mind the meaning of some of the key terms of past scriptures as decoded in Bahá'í writings:

- *Hell, fire, or hell-fire*: Not literal fire, but remoteness from God; the burning desire to come near God.

- *Resurrection*: Each person can experience two resurrections: receive a new life on earth by accepting the Redeemer of the Age and a new life hereafter as a result of that acceptance. The light of faith here gives the soul the true life, the spiritual life. At death, the soul again rises to a new and higher dimension of life. Without faith, the soul remains in the depths of darkness both in this world and the next.

- *Eternity*: Although all souls grow in the next world; the consequences of the choices made here are everlasting. The consequences of remoteness from God (hell) or nearness to God (heaven) will continue from here into the hereafter for all eternity.

- *Death*: All sacred scriptures use the word death to refer not only to physical death but also to spiritual death.

The translation and verse numbering used here is that of Rodwell, although I have changed some of his phrasing to make for easier reading. The numbering of Qur'ánic verses differs in different translations.

Various Teachings of the Qur'án About an Afterlife

This World Created For a Serious Purpose

They know the outward shows of this life present, but of the next life are they careless. Have they not considered within themselves that God hath not created the heavens and the earth and all that is between them but for a serious end, and for a fixed term? But truly most men believe not that they shall meet their Lord. 30:6-7

* * *

It is He who hath appointed the sun for brightness, and the moon for a light, and hath ordained her stations that ye may learn the number of years and the reckoning of time. God hath not created all this but for the truth. He maketh his signs clear to those who understand. Verily, in the alternations of night and of day, and in all that God hath created in the heavens and in the earth are signs to those who fear Him. 10:5-6

This Life a Test

And the life of this world is but a cheating fruition [an illusion]. Ye shall assuredly be tried in your possessions and in your selves. 3:183

* * *

At no time have we granted to man a life that shall last for ever...Every soul shall taste of death: and we will test you

with evil and with good; and unto Us shall ye be brought
back.   21:35-36

Everything Will Come to Light

O my son! Verily God will bring everything to light, though
it were but the weight of a grain of mustard-seed, and hidden
in a rock or in the heavens or in the earth; for, God is subtle,
informed of all.   31:15

God Will Quicken the Dead

Look then at God's mercy—how after its death he quick-
eneth the earth! This same God will surely quicken the
dead.   30:49

Birth Into the Next Life

Say, Go through the earth, and see how He [God] hath
brought forth created beings. Hereafter, will God cause
them to be born again, for God is Almighty.   29:19

Death Inevitable

Wherever ye be, death will overtake you—even ye be in lofty
towers!   4:80

* * *

That Hour is nearer to thee and nearer. It is ever nearer to
thee and nearer still.   75:34-35

Life and Death in God's Hand

He maketh alive and He causeth to die, and to Him shall ye
return.   10:5

* * *

No one can die except by God's permission, according to
the Book that fixeth the term of life.   3:139

The Future Mansion

This present life is no other than vanity and play, but truly
the future mansion is life indeed! Would that they knew
this!   29:64

* * *

As to the future mansion, we will bestow it on those who
seek not to exalt themselves in the earth or to do wrong.
And there is a happy ending for the God-fearing.   28:94

Vying for Pardon and Paradise

Vie in haste after pardon from your Lord, and Paradise—
which is as vast as the heaven and the earth. Prepared is it
for those who believe in God and His Messengers. Such is
the bounty of God, to whom He will He giveth it, and of
immense bounty is God!   57:21

The Way to Paradise

Neither by your riches nor by your children shall you bring
yourselves into nearness with Us [God]; but they who believe
and do the thing that is right shall have a double reward for

what they shall have done, and in the pavilions of Paradise
shall they dwell secure!   34:36

* * *

If ye avoid the great sins which ye are forbidden, we will
erase your faults, and we will cause you to enter paradise
with honorable entry.   4:35

The State of the People of Paradise

Rivers shall flow at their feet in gardens of delight. Their
cry therein, "Glory be to thee, O God!" And their salutation
therein, "Peace!" And the close of their cry, "Praise be to
God, Lord of all creatures!"   10:9-11

Blind Here And Hereafter

And he who has been [spiritually] blind here, shall be blind
hereafter.   17:73

Return From Next Life Impossible

When death overtaketh one of the wicked, he saith, "Lord,
send me back again, that I may do the good which I have
left undone." "By no means!"   23:101-102

The Desire to Return
to This World

Couldst thou but see when the guilty shall bow their heads
before their Lord, and cry, "O our Lord! We have seen and
we have heard, return us then to life, we will do that which
is right. Verily we believe firmly!"   32:12

And therein [in hell] shall they cry aloud, "Take us hence, O our Lord! Righteousness will we work, and not what we did of old." 35:34

* * *

And when they beheld our vengeance they said, "We believe in God alone, and we disbelieve in the deities we once associated with Him." But their faith, after they had witnessed our vengeance, profited them not. 40:84-85

The Gratefulness of the People of Paradise

And they shall say, "Praise be to God who hath put away sorrow from us. Verily our Lord is Gracious, Grateful, who of His bounty hath placed us in a mansion that shall endure for ever, therein no toil shall reach us, and therein no weariness shall touch us." 35:31-32

The Conversation Between the People of Paradise and Hell

On that day the hypocrites, both men and women, shall say to those who believe, "Wait for us, that we may borrow light from your light." It shall be said, "go back behind you, and seek light." Between them shall be set a wall with a gateway, within which shall be the Mercy, and in front and without it, the Torment. They shall cry to them, "Were we not with you?" They shall say, "yes! But ye led yourselves into temptation, and ye delayed, and ye doubted, and the good things ye craved deceived you, until God's judgment came." On that day, therefore, no ransom shall be taken from you or from those who believe not:—your abode the fire! That shall be your master! 57:13-14

The Impassable Barrier

On the day when they shall see the angels, no good news shall there be for the guilty ones, and they shall cry out, "A barrier that cannot be passed!"*   25:24

Storing Treasures For the Future Life

O ye who believe! Fear God. And let every soul look well to what it sendeth on for the morrow...Verily, God is cognizant of what ye do.   59:17-18

Being Charitable
Before Losing the Chance

Give for the cause of God out of that with which we have supplied you, before death surprise each one of you, and you say, "O Lord! Wilt thou not respite me to a term not far distant, that I may give alms, and become one of the just?" And by no means will God respite a soul when its hour hath come! And God is fully cognizant of what ye do.
63:10-11

On the Day of Resurrection

Neither your kindred nor your children shall at all avail you on the day of the resurrection. You will be separated! And your actions doth God behold.   60:4

* * *

---

*...there is a great chasm fixed between us...   Christ (Luke 16:26)

O men! Fear ye your Lord, and dread the day whereon father shall not atone for son, neither shall a son in the least atone for his father. 31:32

* * *

None shall have power to intercede, save he who hath received permission at the hands of the God of Mercy. 19:90

The Stubborn Doubters

But the infidels will not cease to doubt concerning it, until "the Hour" come suddenly upon them, or until the chastisement of the day of desolation come upon them. On that day the Kingdom shall be God's. He shall judge between them, and they who shall have believed and done the things that are right, shall be in gardens of delight. But they who were infidels and treated our signs [proofs and prophecies] as lies— for these then—there is a shameful chastisement! 22:54-56

In the End They Shall Know

And one saith, "O Lord! verily these are people who believe not." Turn thou then from them [don't bother them or condemn them], and say to them, "Peace!" In the end they shall know their folly. 4:88-89

Turning to God

O Believers! Turn to God with true repentance; haply your Lord will cancel your evil deeds, and will bring you into the gardens in which the rivers flow, on the day when God will not shame the Prophet, nor those who have shared His faith. Their light shall run before them, and on their right

hands! They shall say, "Lord perfect our light, and pardon
us, for thou hast power over all things."   66:8

The Great Bounty

One day thou shalt see the believers, men and women, with
their light glowing before them, and on their right hand.
The angels shall say to them, "Good tidings for you this day
of gardens in whose shades the rivers flow, in which ye shall
abide for ever!" This the great bounty!   57:12

Making an Exclusive Claim
to Paradise

Say: If the future dwelling place with God be specially for
you but not for the rest of mankind, then wish for death, if
ye are sincere. But never can they wish for it, because of
that which their own hands have sent on before them! And
God knoweth the offenders.   2:88-89

* * *

And they say, "None but Jews or Christians shall enter Paradise":
This is their wish. Say: Give your proofs if ye speak the
truth.   2:105

Death at a Fixed Time

God taketh souls unto Himself at death; and during their
sleep those who do not die, and he retaineth those on
which he hath passed a decree of death, but sendeth the
others back till a time that is fixed. Herein are signs for the
reflecting.   39:43

Life Review

It is He who taketh your souls at night [during sleep], and knoweth what ye have merited in the day; then he awaketh you therein that the set life-term may be fulfilled; then unto Him shall ye return; and then shall he declare to you that which ye have done.   6:60

What Is Spirit?

And they will ask thee of the spirit. Say: The spirit proceedeth at my Lord's command; but of [that] knowledge, only a little is given to you.*   17:8

God the Refuge

Say: What think ye? If the punishment of God came upon you, or "the Hour"...will ye cry to any other than God? Tell me, if ye speak the truth? Yes! to Him will ye cry, and if He please He will deliver you from that ye shall cry to Him to avert.   6:40-41

Personal Accountability

The soul burdened with its own works shall not be burdened with the burden of another. Hereafter shall ye return to your Lord, and he will tell you of all your works, for he knoweth the very secrets of your hearts.   39:9-10

What Is the Soul?
*"It is a divine energy, a substance, simple, and self-subsistent....it is the Most Sublime Essence of God"[1]

Imám 'Alí, the appointed successor to Muhammad

Knowledge of Afterlife

Say: None either in the heavens or in the earth knoweth the unseen but God. And they know not when they shall be raised. Yet they have attained to a knowledge of the life to come.   27:6-8

Meeting the Lord

And they say, "What! When we shall have lain hidden in the earth, shall we become a new creation?" Yea, they deny that they shall meet their Lord. Say: The angel of death who is charged with you shall cause you to die, then shall ye be returned to your Lord.   32:9-11

God, the Forgiving

Oh! Ye plead in their favor in this present life; but who shall plead with God for them on the day of the resurrection [at death]? Who will be the guardian over them? Yet he who doth evil...and then shall ask pardon of God, will find God forgiving and merciful.   4:109-110

Freedom of Choice

He who desireth the recompense of this world, we will give him thereof: And he who desireth the recompense of the next life, we will give him thereof! And we will certainly reward the thankful.   3:139

Deniers Afflicted by Delusion

And for those who believe not in their Lord is the torment
of hell; and horrid the journey thither!...So oft as a crowd
shall be thrown into it, its keepers shall ask them, "Came
not the Warner [Messenger] to you?" They shall say, yes!
There came to us one charged with warnings; but we treated
Him as a liar, and said, "Nothing hath God sent down; ye
are in nothing but a vast delusion." And they shall say,
"Had we but hearkened or understood, we would not be
the dwellers in the flames."   67:6-11

God's Bounties For Martyrs

And think not those slain in God's path to be dead. Alive
with their Lord, they are richly sustained, rejoicing in what
God of his bounty hath bestowed on them. They are filled
with joy for those who follow them—those on whom there
is no fear or grief. They will rejoice in the blessings bestowed
on them. God allows not the reward of the faithful to perish.
                                                      3:169-171

Humans Accountable

By God ye shall be called to account for your doings! 16:58

Purity

And whoever shall keep himself pure, he purifieth himself
for his own good. Unto God shall be the final gathering.
                                                        35:19

A Prayer

O our Lord! Thou embracest all things in mercy and knowledge; forgive, therefore, those who turn to thee and follow thy path; keep them from the pains of hell. O our Lord! Bring them into the Gardens of Eden which thou hast promised to them, and to the righteous ones of their fathers and their wives and their children; for thou art the All-mighty, the All-wise. And keep them from evil, for on him hast thou mercy whom on that day thou shalt keep from evil; and this will be the great victory.   40:7-9

Return to God

Unto Him Shall Ye Return

Unto me [God] shall ye return at last, and then will I tell you of your doings.   31:14

* * *

Unto Him shall ye return, all together; the promise of God is sure. He produceth a creature, then causeth it to return [to Him] again—that he may reward equitably those who believe and do the things that are right.   10:4

Attaining Old Age

And God hath created you; bye and bye will he take you to himself; and some among you will he carry on to old age, when all that once was known is known no longer. Aye, God is Knowing, Powerful.   16:72

A Home in Heaven

Every soul shall taste of death. Then to Us shall ye return. Those who believe and do works of righteousness shall be given a home in heaven, and mansions beneath which the rivers flow. For ever shall they abide therein.   29:57-58

God's Nearness to the Dying

When ye are gazing at him [a dying person], though we are nearer to him than ye, ye see us not...   56:83-84

Sovereignty of God

Verily, We will inherit the earth and all who are upon it. To Us shall they be brought back.   19:11

On the Day of Resurrection

Verily there is none in the heavens and in the earth but shall approach the God of Mercy as a servant...Each of them shall come to Him, on the day of Resurrection, singly. Love will the God of Mercy bestow to those who believe and do the right things.   19:94-96

All Deeds Recorded

Verily, it is We who will quicken the dead, and write down the works which they have sent on before them, and the traces which they shall have left behind them. Everything have we set down in the clear Book of our decrees.   36:11

* * *

And each shall have his book put into his hand; and thou shalt see the wicked in alarm at that which is therein, and they shall say, "O woe to us! What meaneth this Book? It leaveth neither small nor great unnoted!" And they shall find all that they have done placed before them. Thy Lord will not deal unjustly with any one.   18:47

* * *

Whatever good works ye send on before [death]...ye shall find with God.   31:20

* * *

And every man's fate have we fastened around his neck. And on the day of resurrection will we bring forth to him a Book which shall be offered to him wide open: "Read thy Book; none is needed but thyself to make out an account against thee this day."   17:14-15

* * *

One day We will summon all people with their leaders. They whose book shall be given into their right hand, shall read their book, and not be wronged a thread.   17:73

* * *

And their own ill deeds shall be clearly perceived by them, and that fire at which they mocked shall encircle them on every side.   39:49

* * *

On that day when God shall raise them all to life, and shall tell them of their doings. God hath taken count of them, though they have forgotten them! And God is witness over all things.   58:7

* * *

Is not whatever is in the heavens and the earth God's? He knoweth your state; and one day shall people be assembled before Him, and He will tell them of what they have done, for God knoweth all things.   24:64

* * *

And whoso shall do the things that are right, and be a believer, his efforts shall not be disowned; and surely will we write them down for him.   21:94

* * *

Verily, we warn you of a chastisement close at hand: The day on which a man shall see the deeds which his hands have set before him; and when the unbeliever shall say, "Oh! Would I were dust!"   78:40-41

* * *

God will behold your work, and so will His Messenger, and the faithful. And ye shall be brought before Him who knoweth alike the hidden and the manifest, and He will tell you of all your works.   9:106

The Soul's Reluctance to Review Bad Deeds

On that day shall every soul find present before it whatever it hath done of good. As to what it hath done of evil, it will wish that wide were the space between itself and it!   3:28

The Day of Reckoning

On a certain day shall every soul come to plead for itself, and every soul shall be repaid according to its deeds; and they shall not be wronged.   16:112

The Day of Reward

Fear the day wherein ye shall return to God; then every soul shall be rewarded according to its merits, and none shall be treated unjustly.   2:281

Prayer for Forgiveness

O our Lord! Forgive me and my parents and the faithful,
on the day wherein account shall be taken.   14:112

Angels

Praise be to God, Maker of the heavens and of the earth,
who appoints the angels as envoys.   34:1

***

Truly there are guardians over you—illustrious recorders—
cognizant of your actions.   82:10-12

***

They [angels] speak not till He hath spoken; and they do
His bidding. He knoweth what is before them and what is
behind them; and no plea shall they offer save for whom
He pleaseth; and they tremble for fear of Him.   21:27-29

***

As for those who say, "Our Lord is God," then pursue a
righteous life, the angels shall descend on them and say,
"Fear ye not, neither be ye grieved, but rejoice in the paradise
which ye have been promised. We are your guardians in this
life and in the next: yours therein shall be your soul's desire,
and yours therein whatever ye shall ask for."   41:30-31

***

Supreme over His servants, He sendeth forth guardians
who watch over you, until, when death overtaketh any one
of you, His messengers take your soul, and fail not. Then
are they returned to God their Lord, the True. Is not judgment
His? Swiftest is He, of those who take account!   6:61-62

***

Each hath a succession of angels before him and behind him, who watch over him by God's behest.   13:12

***

By His own behest He will cause the angels to descend with the Spirit on whom he pleaseth among his servants, bidding them, "Warn that there is no God but me; therefore fear me."   16:2

***

The [angels who] snatch [the souls of the wicked] forcibly. And the angels who gently take [the souls of the noble] joyfully. And those [angels who] float along, eagerly racing—to carry out the affairs of the universe.   79:1-5

***

All beings in the heaven and on the earth are His; and they who are in his presence disdain not his service, neither are they wearied; they praise Him night and day; they rest not.

21:19-20

***

O Believers! Save yourselves and your families from the fire whose fuel is men and stones, over which are set angels fierce and mighty. They disobey not God in what He hath commanded them, but execute His behests.   66:6

***

Over every soul is set a guardian.   86:4

***

He blesseth you, and His angels intercede for you, that He may bring you forth out of darkness into light; and Merciful is He to the believers.   33:12

***

This is the word of an illustrious Messenger, endowed with power, having influence with the Lord of the Throne, obeyed there by angels, faithful to His trust.   81:19-21

***

And they consider the angels who are the servants of God
of Mercy, females. What! Did they witness their creation?

43:18

***

Praise be to God, Maker of the heavens and of the earth,
who employeth the angels as envoys, with pairs of wings,
two, three, and four. He addeth to His creature what He
will! Truly God hath power for all things.   35:1

Descriptions of Heaven And Hell

Peace in the Garden of Eden

The Garden of Eden, which the God of Mercy hath promised
to his servants, though yet unseen, shall come to pass. No
vain discourse shall they hear therein, but only "Peace;" and
their food shall be given them at morn and even. This is the
Paradise which we will make the heritage of those servants
who fear us.   19:62-64

Deeds That Lead to Paradise

But the God-fearing shall dwell amid gardens and fountains,
enjoying what their Lord hath given them, because [while
on earth] they were well-doers. Little of the night was it that
they slept, and at dawn they prayed for pardon. And they
gave due share of their wealth to the needy and the outcast.

51:15-19

An Image of Paradise

A picture of the paradise, which God hath promised to those who fear Him. The rivers flow beneath its bowers; its food and its shades are perpetual. This is the reward of those who fear God; but the reward of the unbelievers is the Fire. 13:35

Who Will Dwell in Paradise?

But as to those who have believed and done the things which are right—we will lay on no one a burden beyond his power. These shall be inmates of paradise; for ever shall they abide therein; and we will remove whatever rancor was in their hearts. Rivers shall roll at their feet, and they shall say, "Praise be to God who hath guided us hither! We would not be guided had God not guided us! Of a certainty the Messengers of our Lord came to us with truth." And a voice shall cry to them, "This is paradise, of which, as the result of your works, ye are made heirs." 7:42-43

The Abode of the Pious

But amidst gardens and fountains shall the pious dwell: "Enter ye therein in peace, secure." And all rancor [unworthy feelings] will We remove from their hearts. They shall sit as brethren, face to face, on couches. Therein no weariness shall reach them, nor from it shall they ever be cast out. 15:46-48

Faith And Good Deeds Required
For Entering Paradise

And whoever believeth in God, and doeth the things that are right, God will cause him to enter the gardens in which the rivers flow, to remain therein for ever! A goodly provision now hath God made for him.   65:11

* * *

Verily God will bring those who believe and do the things that are right into the Gardens, beneath whose shades the rivers flow.   47:13

* * *

They who believe and do the things that are right shall dwell in the meadows of paradise; whatever they shall desire awaiteth them with their Lord. This, the greatest bounty. This is what God announceth to His servants who believe and do the things that are right.   42:21-22

The Soul's Destiny

Oh, thou soul which are at rest, return to thy Lord, pleased, and pleasing him: Enter thou among my servants, and enter thou my Paradise.   89:27-30

Choosing One's Harvest Field

Whoever chooseth the harvest field of the life to come, to him will we give increase in that harvest field; and whoever chooseth the harvest field of this life, thereof will we give him. But no portion shall there be for him in the life to come.   42:19

Punishment of the Unjust

And thou shalt behold the perpetrators of injustice, exclaiming, when they see the torment, "Is there no way to return?" And thou shalt see them when set before the torment downcast for the shame; they shall look at it with stealthy glances. And the believers shall say, "Truly are the losers they who have lost themselves and their families on the day of Resurrection! Shall not the perpetrators of injustice be in lasting torment?" And no other protectors shall there be to support them than God; and no pathway for him whom God shall allow to err. Listen then to your Lord before the day comes, which none can put back when God doth ordain its coming. No place of refuge for you on that day! No denying your own works!   42:42-46

Terrible Retribution

If those who transgressed owned everything on earth, even twice as much, they would readily give it up to avoid the terrible retribution of the Day of Resurrection. They will be shown by God what they never expected. The sinful works they had earned will be shown to them, and the very things they used to mock will come back to haunt them.   39:47-48 R

Joys For the Good

No soul knoweth the joy of the eyes reserved for the good as rewards of their works.   32:17

Fire For the Wicked

On a certain day, God shall say, "Call ye on the companions ye joined with Me, regarding them as gods." And they shall call on them, but they shall not answer...And the wicked

shall see the fire, and shall realize that they shall be flung
into it, and they shall find no escape from it.   18:50-51

Grief in Hell

And as for those who shall be consigned to misery—their
place the Fire! Therein shall they sigh and bemoan. Therein
shall they abide while the heavens and the earth shall last,
unless thy Lord shall will it otherwise; verily thy Lord doth
what He chooseth.   11:108-109

Gardens For the Faithful

But they who shall have believed and done the things that
be right, shall be brought into gardens in which the rivers
flow. Therein shall they abide for ever by the permission of
their Lord; their greeting therein shall be "Peace."   14:28

Chastisement

Chastisement awaiteth them in this present life, and more
grievous shall be the chastisement of the next. And none
shall protect them against God.   13:34

* * *

And God made them taste humiliation in this present life;
but greater surely will be the punishment of the life to
come. Did they but know it!   39:27

The Obedient And
the Prophets Together

And whoever shall obey God and the Messengers, these shall be with those blessed by God, among them the prophets, the saints, the martyrs, and the righteous, to whom God hath been gracious. These are a goodly group! Such is the bounty of God; and His knowledge sufficeth.   4:71-72

In the Presence of the Lord

Verily, for the God-fearing are gardens of delight in the presence of their Lord.   68:34

The Ways to Hell

While in paradise, they [the saints] shall ask of the wicked; "What hath cast you into hell-fire?" They will say, "We were not of those who prayed, and we were not of those who fed the poor, and we engaged in vain disputes with vain disputers, and we rejected as a lie the day of reckoning, till the certainty came upon us."   74:42-48

* * *

Verily, they who hope not to meet Us, and who find their satisfaction in the earthly life, and rest in it, and who of our signs are heedless; their abode shall be the fire.   10:7-8

Just Balance

Just balances will we set up for the day of the resurrection. No soul shall be wronged even as little as the weight of a grain of mustard seed. We will bring it forth to be weighed, and our reckoning will suffice.   21:48

The Reward of the Blessed

And as for the blessed ones—their place the Garden! Therein shall they abide while the heavens and the earth endure, with whatever imperishable bounties thy Lord may please to add.   11:110

The State of the People of Hell

And a gulf shall be between them and that which they shall desire.   34:53

Receiving One's Desire

Those who believe and do the things that are right...whatever they shall desire awaiteth them with their Lord. This, the greatest bounty.   42:21-22

Levels of Heaven and Hell

Seven Levels of Hell

It hath seven Portals; at each Portal is a separate band of them...   15:44

Various Gardens

Shall he who hath followed the good pleasure of God be as he who hath brought on himself wrath from God, and whose abode shall be Hell? And wretched the journey there!

There are varying gardens with God, and God beholdeth
what ye do.   3:156-157

The Day of Separation

And the infidels shall be gathered together into hell, that
God may separate the bad from the good, and put the bad
one upon the other...These are they who shall be lost.

8:37-38

Grades of Reward

And for all are grades of reward as the result of their deeds;
and of what they do, thy Lord is not regardless.   6:132

A Comparison Between
Earthly Life and Heavenly

The Meager Fruits of This Life

What! Prefer ye the life of this world to the next? But the
fruits of this mundane life, compared to that which shall
come, is but little.   9:38

True Life in the Future Mansion

This present life is no other than a vanity and a play, but
truly the future mansion is life indeed! Would that they
knew this!   29:64

Earthly Life Temporary

The analogy of this worldly life is like this: we send down water from the sky to produce all kinds of plants from the earth, and to provide food for the people and the animals. Then, just as the earth is perfectly adorned, and its people think that they are in control thereof, our judgment comes by night or by day, rendering it completely barren, as if nothing existed the previous day. We thus explain the revelations for people who reflect.   10:24 R

Keeping the Covenant

And barter not the covenant of God for a mean price; for with God is that which is better for you, if ye do but understand. All that is with you passeth away, but that which is with God abideth. With a reward fit for their best deeds will we surely repay those who have patiently endured. 16:97-98

Withdrawal From the Worldly

Withdraw then from him who turneth his back on our warning and desireth only this present life.   53:30

Building on God or on Sand

Which of the two is best? He who hath built on the fear of God and the desire to please Him, or he who hath built on the brink of an undermined bank washed away by torrents, so that it rusheth with him into the fire of hell? God guideth not the doers of wrong.   9:110-111

Next Life Better

Ye prefer this present life, though the life to come is better and more enduring. This truly is in the Books of old, the Books of Abraham and Moses. 87:16-19

* * *

And all that hath been bestowed on you is merely for enjoyment and pomp of this life present, but that which is with God is better and more lasting. Will ye not be wise? 28:60

* * *

Ye desire the passing fruits of this world, but God desireth the next life for you. And God is Mighty, Wise. 8:68

The Good of Both This Life and the Next

Some say, "O our Lord! Give us our portion in this world." But such shall have no portion in the next life. And others say, "O our Lord! Give us good in this world and good in the next, and keep us from the torment of the fire." They shall have the destiny which they have merited, and God is swift to reckon. 2:147-148

This Life a Play and Pastime

The life in this world is but a play and pastime; and better surely for the righteous will be the future mansion! Will ye not then comprehend? 6:32

A Place of Play

Know ye that this life is only a show, a place of play, vanity, and pride. And the multiplying of riches and children is like the plants which spring up after rain. Their growth rejoiceth the former; then they wither away, and thou seest them all yellow, then they become stubble.   57:19

Waste of Precious Gifts

And they who believe not shall one day be set before the fire. "Ye wasted your precious gifts during your life on earth; and took pleasure in what you did. This day, therefore, with punishment of shame shall ye be rewarded, for ye behaved proudly and unjustly on the earth, and ye were given to excesses."   46:19

Danger of Deception

The promise of God is a truth. Let not this present life then deceive you; neither let the deceiver deceive you concerning God.   31:33

Self-Deception

And they say, "There is only this our present life. We die and we live, and nought but time destroyeth us." But they have no knowledge. It is merely their own conceit.   45:23

A Passing Good

They rejoice in the life that now is, but this present life is but a passing good, in comparison to the life to come!   13:26

Parable of Present Life

And set before them a parable about the present life. It is as water which we send down from heaven, and the herb of the earth is mingled with it, and tomorrow it becometh dry stubble which the winds scatter.   18:43

The Deceptive Appearances

None but infidels deny the signs of God, but let not their prosperity in the land deceive thee.   40:4

No Eternal Life For the Worldly

Those who choose this present life and its worldly vanities... These are they for whom there is nothing in the next world but the fire. All that they have done in this life shall come to nought, and vain shall be all their doings.   11:18-19

Next Life Greater in Grades And in Excellence

See how we have caused some of them to excel others! But the next life shall be greater in its grades, and greater in excellence.   17:22

Results of Choices

Those who choose this quickly passing life, quickly will we bestow on them therein that which we please. But those who choose the next life, and strive after it as it should be striven for, being also a believer—these shall enjoy the fruits of their works.   17:19-21

Desire for Riches and Pleasures

The desire for increasing riches occupieth you, till ye come to the grave. Nay! But in the end ye shall know. Nay! Once more, in the end ye shall know your folly. Nay! Would that ye knew it with knowledge of certainty! Surely ye shall see hell-fire. Then shall ye surely see it with the eye of certainty. Then shall ye on that day be taken to task concerning pleasures.
102:1-8

True Wisdom

And all that hath been bestowed on you is merely for enjoyment and pomp of this life present. But that which is with God is better and more lasting. Will ye not be wise?   28:60

Part VI

Selections From
the New Testament
(New International Version)

Fulfilling One's Mission

I desire to depart and be with Christ, which is better by far; but it is more necessary for you that I remain in the body. Convinced of this, I know that I will remain, and I will continue with all of you for your progress and joy in the faith...   Philippians 1:23-24

At Home With the Lord

As long as we are at home in the body we are away from the Lord...and would prefer to be away from the body and at home with the Lord.   II Corinthians 5:6-9

Reunion in Paradise

One of criminals who hung there hurled insults at him: "Aren't you the Christ? Save yourself and us!" But the other criminal rebuked him. "Don't you fear God," he said, "since you are under the same sentence? We are punished justly, for we are getting what our deeds deserve. But this man has done nothing wrong." Then he said, "Jesus, remember me when you come into your kingdom." Jesus answered him, "I tell you the truth, today you will be with me in paradise."
Luke 23:39-43

True Source of Life

I declare to you, brothers, that flesh and blood cannot inherit the kingdom of God, nor does the perishable inherit the imperishable.   I Corinthians 15:50

* * *

The spirit gives life, the flesh is of no avail.   John 6:63

Looking at the Eternal

So we fix our eyes not on what is seen but on what is unseen.
For what is seen is temporary, but what is unseen is eternal.
                                                    II Corinthians 4:18

Essence of Life

...the body without the spirit is dead...   James 2:26

* * *

Do not be afraid of those who kill the body but cannot kill
the soul. Rather, be afraid of the one who can destroy both
soul and body...   Matthew 10:28

Heavenly Bodies

If the dead are not raised [to another life], "Let us eat and
drink, for tomorrow we die..." But someone may ask, "How
are the dead raised? With what kind of body will they
come?"...There are also heavenly bodies and there are earthly
bodies; but the splendor of the heavenly bodies is one kind,
and the splendor of the earthly bodies is another. The sun
has one kind of splendor, the moon another and the stars
another; and star differs from star in splendor.

So will it be with the resurrection of the dead. The body
that is sown is perishable, it is raised imperishable; it is
sown in dishonor, it is raised in glory; it is sown in weakness, it is raised in power; it is sown a natural body, it is
raised a spiritual body. If there is a natural body, there is
also a spiritual body...And just as we have borne the likeness

of the earthly man, so shall we bear the likeness of the man from heaven. I declare to you, brothers, that flesh and blood cannot inherit the kingdom of God, nor does the perishable inherit the imperishable.   I Corinthians 15:32-50

God's Sight

Nothing in all creation is hidden from God's sight. Everything is uncovered and laid bare before the eyes of him to whom we must give account.   Hebrews 4:13

Day of Judgment

The sea gave up the dead that were in it, and death and Hades gave up the dead that were in them, and each person was judged according to what he had done. Revelation 20:13

Judgment Seat

For we will all stand before God's judgment seat. It is written: "As surely as I live," says the Lord, "Every knee will bow before me; every tongue will confess to God."

Romans 14:10-11

The Day of Reckoning

For we must all appear before the judgment seat of Christ, that each one may receive what is due him for the things done while in the body, whether good or bad.

II Corinthians 5:10

The Impassable Chasm

There was a rich man who was dressed in purple and fine linen and lived in luxury every day. At his gate was laid a beggar named Lazarus, covered with sores and longing to eat what fell from the rich man's table. Even the dogs came and licked his sores. The time came when the beggar died and the angels carried him to Abraham's side. The rich man also died and was buried. In hell, where he was in torment, he looked up and saw Abraham far away, with Lazarus by his side. So he called to him, 'Father Abraham, have pity on me and send Lazarus to dip the tip of his finger in water and cool my tongue, because I am in agony in this fire.' But Abraham replied, 'Son, remember that in your lifetime you received your good things, while Lazarus received bad things, but now he is comforted here and you are in agony. And besides all this, between us and you a great chasm has been fixed, so that those who want to go from here to you cannot, nor can anyone cross over from there to us.' He answered, 'Then I beg you, father, send Lazarus to my father's house, for I have five brothers. Let him warn them, so that they will not also come to this place of torment.' Abraham replied, 'They have Moses and the Prophets; let them listen to them.' 'No, father Abraham,' he said, 'but if someone from the dead goes to them, they will repent.' He said to him, 'If they do not listen to Moses and the Prophets, they will not be convinced even if someone rises from the dead.'

Luke 16:19-31

Nearness to Christ Must Be Earned

...but to sit at my right or left is not for me to grant. These places belong to those for whom they have been prepared.

Mark 10:40

Rewards of Faith And Suffering

For our light and momentary troubles are achieving for us an eternal glory that far outweighs them all.

II Corinthians 4:17

Consequence Inevitable

I will give you the keys of the kingdom of heaven; whatever you bind on earth will be bound in heaven, and whatever you loose on earth will be loosed in heaven.   Matthew 16:19

Attachment to Wealth

...it is hard for a rich man to enter the kingdom of heaven. Again I tell you, it is easier for a camel to go through the eye of a needle than for a rich man to enter the kingdom of God.   Matthew 19:23-24

Eternal Life Dependent on Faith and Good Deeds

If you want to enter life, obey the commandments.

Matthew 19:21

* * *

...everyone who believes in him may have eternal life.

John 3:15

* * *

...whoever hears my word and believes him who sent me has eternal life and will not be condemned; he has crossed over from death to life.   John 5:24

* * *

...if a man keeps my word, he will never see death.

John 8·51

* * *

I am the resurrection and the life. He who believes in me will live, even though he dies; and whoever lives and believes in me will never die.   John 11:25-26

* * *

The one who sows to please his sinful nature, from that nature will reap destruction; the one who sows to please the Spirit, from the Spirit will reap eternal life.   Galatians 6:8

* * *

The world and its desires pass away, but the man who does the will of God lives forever.   I John 2:17

* * *

Be faithful, even to the point of death, and I will give you the crown of life.   Revelation 2:10

Reward Measured to Deeds

God will give to each person according to what he has done.   Romans 2:6

Many Mansions

In my Father's house are many mansions; if it were not so, I would have told you. I go to prepare a place for you. And if I go and prepare a place for you, I will come again and receive you to Myself; that where I am, there you may be also. And where I go you know, and the way you know.

John 14:2-4

* * *

Simon Peter asked him, "Lord, where are you going?" Jesus replied, "Where I am going, you cannot follow now, but you will follow later."   John 13:36

Humility the Key to Heaven

I tell the truth, unless you change and become like little children, you will never enter the kingdom of heaven. Therefore, whoever humbles himself like this child is the greatest in the kingdom of heaven.   Matthew 18:3-4

* * *

I tell you the truth, anyone who will not receive the kingdom of God like a little child will never enter it.   Mark 10:15

* * *

Blessed are the poor in spirit, for theirs is the kingdom of heaven.   Matthew 5:3

An Eternal House in Heaven

Now we know that if the earthly tent we live in is destroyed, we have a building from God, an eternal house in heaven, not built by human hands.   II Corinthians 4:1

Wicked Will Not Inherit the Kingdom

Do you not know that the wicked will not inherit the kingdom of God? Do not be deceived: Neither the sexually immoral nor idolaters nor adulterers nor male prostitutes nor homosexual offenders nor thieves nor the greedy nor drunkards nor slanderers nor swindlers will inherit the kingdom of God.
                                        I Corinthians 6:9-10

The First Shall Be the Last

Make every effort to enter through the narrow door, because many, I tell you, will try to enter and will not be able to. Once the owner of the house gets up and closes the door, you will stand outside knocking and pleading, 'Sir, open the door for us.' But he will answer, 'I don't know you or where you come from.' Then you will say, 'We ate and drank with you, and you taught in our streets.' But he will reply, 'I don't know you or where you come from. Away from me, all you evildoers!' There will be weeping there, and gnashing of teeth, when you see Abraham, Isaac and Jacob and all the prophets in the kingdom of God, but you yourselves thrown out. People will come from east and west and north and south, and will take their places at the feast in the kingdom of God. Indeed there are those who are last who will be first, and first who will be last.

Luke 13:24-30

Book of Life

If anyone's name was not found written in the book of life, he was thrown into the lake of fire.   Revelation 20:15

Avoiding Hell

It is better for you to enter the kingdom of God with one eye than to have two eyes and be thrown into hell...

Mark 9:47

Meaning of Life and Death

"...there is rejoicing in the presence of the angels of God over one sinner who repents." Jesus continued: "There was a man who had two sons. The younger one said to his father, 'Father, give me my share of the estate.' So he divided his property between them. Not long after that, the younger son got together all he had, set off for a distant country and there squandered his wealth in wild living. After he had spent everything, there was a severe famine in that whole country, and he began to be in need. So he went and hired himself out to a citizen of that country, who sent him to his fields to feed pigs. He longed to fill his stomach with the pods that the pigs were eating, but no one gave him anything. When he came to his senses, he said, 'How many of my father's hired men have food to spare, and here I am starving to death! I will set out and go back to my father and say to him: Father, I have sinned against heaven and against you. I am no longer worthy to be called your son; make me like one of your hired men.' So he got up and went to his father. But while he was still a long way off, his father saw him and was filled with compassion for him; he ran to his son, threw his arms around him and kissed him. The son said to him, 'Father, I have sinned against heaven and against you. I am no longer worthy to be called your son.' But the father said to his servants, 'Quick! Bring the best robe and put it on him. Put a ring on his finger and sandals on his fee. Bring the fattened calf and kill it. Let's have a feast and celebrate. For this son of mine was dead and is alive again; he was lost and is found.' So they began to celebrate."   Luke 15:10-24

Eternal Life

...and they can no longer die; for they are like the angels. They are God's children, since they are children of the resurrection.   Luke 20:36

Rebirth

I tell you the truth, unless a man is born again, he cannot see the kingdom of God.   John 3:3

* * *

I tell you the truth, unless a man is born of water [of life] and the Spirit, he cannot enter the kingdom of God.

John 3:5

Role of Angels

Are not all angels ministering spirits sent to serve those who will inherit salvation?   Hebrews 1:14

Brevity of This Life

All men are like grass, and all their glory is like the flowers of the field; the grass withers and the flowers fall...

I Peter 1:24

Losing One's Soul

What good will it be for a man if he gains the whole world, yet forfeits his soul? Or what can a man give in exchange for his soul?   Matthew 16:26

Seeking the Eternal

Do not work for food that spoils, but for food that endures to eternal life, which the Son of Man will give you. On him God the Father has placed his seal of approval.

John 6:27

Exchanging Everything For the Heavenly Kingdom

The kingdom of heaven is like treasure hidden in a field. When a man found it, he hid it again, and then in his joy went and sold all he had and bought that field.

Matthew 13:44

Detachment

No one who puts his hand to the plow and looks back is fit for service in the kingdom of God.

Luke 9:62

Seeking God's Kingdom

But seek his kingdom, and these [worldly] things will be given to you as well. Do not be afraid, little flock, for your Father has been pleased to give you the kingdom.

Luke 12:31-32

Losing This Life For the Next

For whoever wants to save his life will lose, but whoever loses his life for me will find it.

Matthew 16:25

Everything For God's Sake

If we live, we live to the Lord; and if we die, we die to the Lord. So, whether we live or die, we belong to the Lord.

Romans 14:8

Part VII

Selections From
the Old Testament
(New International Version)

A Time For Everything

...a time to be born and a time to die, a time to plant and a time to uproot.   Ecclesiastes 3:2

Death Even Better Than Birth

A good name is better than fine perfume, and the day of death better than the day of birth.   Ecclesiastes 7:1

The Glory of Being Human

When I consider your heavens, the work of your fingers, the moon and the stars, which you have set in place, what is man that you are mindful of him, the son of man that you care for him? You made him a little lower than the heavenly beings and crowned him with glory and honor. You made him ruler over the works of your hands; you put everything under his feet...   Psalms 8:3-6

Naked to This World

Naked a man comes from his mother's womb, and as he comes, so he departs. He takes nothing from his labor that he can carry in his hand.   Ecclesiastes 5:15

* * *

Naked I came from my mother's womb, and naked I will depart.   Job 1:20

Return to Dust

Dust you are and to dust you return.   Genesis 3:19

* * *

All come from dust, and to dust all return.   Ecclesiastes 3:20

Return to God

...the dust returns to the ground it came from, and the spirit
returns to God who gave it.   Ecclesiastes 12:7

We Belong to God

Every living soul belongs to me...   Ezekiel 18:4

He Restores My Soul

The Lord is my shepherd, I shall lack nothing. He makes me
lie down in green pastures, he leads me beside quiet waters,
he restores my soul. He guides me in paths of righteousness
for his name's sake. Even though I walk through the valley
of the shadow of death, I will fear no evil, for you are with
me; your rod and your staff, they comfort me. You prepare
a table before me in the presence of my enemies. You
anoint my head with oil; my cup overflows. Surely goodness
and love will follow me all the days of my life, and I will
dwell in the house of the Lord forever.   Psalms 23:1-6

Eternal Pleasures

...you will not abandon me to the grave, nor will you let
your Holy One see decay. You have made known to me the
path of life; you will fill me with joy in your presence, with
eternal pleasures at your right hand.   Psalms 16:10-11

Reunion at Death

...tomorrow you and your sons will be with me.
>   I Samuel 28:19 (Samuel, after his death, to Saul)

A One-Way Journey

Can I bring him back again? I will go to him, but he will
not return to me.   II Samuel 12:23 (David, about his son)

* * *

...he who goes down to the grave does not return.   Job 7:9

* * *

...before I go to the place of no return, to the land of
gloom and deep shadow...   Job 10:21

Mediums

Do not turn to mediums or seek out spirits, for you will be
defiled by them. I am the Lord your God.   Leviticus 19:31

Visions And Dreams

...thou speakest in vision to thy saints...   Psalms 89:19

A Fleeting Shadow

Man is like a breath; his days are like a fleeting shadow.
>   Psalms 144:4

Vanity of Wealth

Do not be overawed when a man grows rich, when the splendor of his house increases; for he will take nothing with him when he dies, his splendor will not descend with him.   Psalms 49:16-17

Consequences of Sin

The soul who sins is the one who will die.*   Ezekiel 18:4

All Perish Except Those Who Love And Trust God

For all can see that wise men die; the foolish and the senseless alike perish and leave their wealth to others. Their tombs will remain their houses forever, their dwelling for endless generations, though they had named lands after themselves. But man, despite his riches, does not endure; he is like the beasts that perish. This is the fate of those who trust in themselves...A man who has riches without understanding is like the beasts that perish.   Psalms 49:1-13,20

Obedience

He who obeys instructions guards his soul, but he who is contemptuous of his ways will die.   Proverbs 19:16

---

*it is evident that everyone dies. Death in all these passages refers to a lack of spiritual life or spiritual deprivation.

God's Love For Everyone

Rid yourselves of all the offenses you have committed, and get a new heart and a new spirit. Why will you die, O house of Israel? For I take no pleasure in the [spiritual] death of anyone, declares the Sovereign Lord. Repent and live!

Ezekiel 18:31-32

Who May Dwell in Divine Sanctuary?

Lord, who may dwell in your sanctuary? Who may live on your holy hill? He whose walk is blameless and who does what is righteous, who speaks the truth from his heart and has no slander on his tongue, who does his neighbor no wrong and casts no slur on his fellow man...who keeps his oath even when it hurts, who lends his money without usury and does not accept a bribe against the innocent. He who does these things will never be shaken. Psalms 15:1-5

Blessed the Pure in Spirit

Blessed is he whose transgressions are forgiven, whose sins are covered. Blessed is the man whose sin the Lord does not count against him and in whose spirit is no deceit.

Psalms 32:1-2

Blessed Are Those Who Dwell in His House

Blessed are those who dwell in your house; they are ever praising you...Better is one day in your courts than a thousand elsewhere...For the Lord God is a sun and shield; the Lord

bestows favor and honor; no good thing does he withhold
from those whose walk is blameless.   Psalms 84:4,10-11

Before the Silver Cord is Severed

Remember him—before the silver cord is severed, or the
golden bowl is broken; before the pitcher is shattered at the
spring, or the wheel broken at the well...   Ecclesiastes 12:6

References

Preface

1. Shoghi Effendi. *The Dispensation of Bahá'u'lláh*, Wilmette, IL: Bahá'í Publishing Committee, 1947, p. 16.

2. *The Kitáb-i-Aqdas*, 1992, p. 49.

3. Shoghi Effendi. *The Promised Day Is Come*, Wilmette, IL: Bahá'í Publishing Committee, 1951, p. 121.

4. Shoghi Effendi. *The Promised Day Is Come*, Wilmette, IL: Bahá'í Publishing Committee, 1951, p. 121.

5. *Gleanings from the Writings of Bahá'u'lláh*, pp. 12-13.

6. *The Proclamation of Bahá'u'lláh*, p. 27.

7. *Tablets of Bahá'u'lláh*, pp. 78-79.

8. *The Kitáb-i-Aqdas*, p. 39.

9. *Gleanings from the Writings of Bahá'u'lláh*, p. 329.

Part I

1. *Gleanings from the Writings of Bahá'u'lláh*, pp. 155-158.

2. *Gleanings from the Writings of Bahá'u'lláh*, pp. 169-171.

3. *Gleanings from the Writings of Bahá'u'lláh*, pp. 151-153.

4. *Gleanings from the Writings of Bahá'u'lláh*, pp. 158-162.

5. *Gleanings from the Writings of Bahá'u'lláh*, p. 65.

6. *Gleanings from the Writings of Bahá'u'lláh*, pp. 77-78.

7. *Gleanings from the Writings of Bahá'u'lláh*, pp. 153-155.

8. *Gleanings from the Writings of Bahá'u'lláh*, pp. 164-165.

9. *The Seven Valleys and the Four Valleys*, pp. 32-33.

10. *Gleanings from the Writings of Bahá'u'lláh*, p. 149.

11. *Gleanings from the Writings of Bahá'u'lláh*, pp. 140-141.

12. *Tablets of Bahá'u'lláh*, p. 220.

13. *Gleanings from the Writings of Bahá'u'lláh*, pp. 177-179.

14. *Gleanings from the Writings of Bahá'u'lláh*, p. 327.

15. *Gleanings from the Writings of Bahá'u'lláh*, pp. 345-346.

16. *Gleanings from the Writings of Bahá'u'lláh*, p. 329.

17. *Tablets of Bahá'u'lláh*, p. 189.

18. *Kitáb-i-Íqán*, p. 118.

19. *Tablets of Bahá'u'lláh*, p. 232.

20. *Gleanings from the Writings of Bahá'u'lláh*, pp. 282-284.

21. *Kitáb-i-Íqán*, pp. 78-80.

22. *Gleanings from the Writings of Bahá'u'lláh*, pp. 70-71.

23. *Gleanings from the Writings of Bahá'u'lláh*, pp. 226-227.

24. *The Hidden Words of Bahá'u'lláh* (Arabic), no. 14.

25. *The Hidden Words of Bahá'u'lláh* (Arabic), no. 32.

26. *The Hidden Words of Bahá'u'lláh* (Arabic), no. 61.

27. *The Hidden Words of Bahá'u'lláh* (Arabic), no. 69.

28. *The Hidden Words of Bahá'u'lláh* (Persian), no. 37.

29. *The Hidden Words of Bahá'u'lláh* (Persian), no. 40.

30. *The Hidden Words of Bahá'u'lláh* (Persian), no. 41.

31. *The Hidden Words of Bahá'u'lláh* (Persian), no. 44.

32. *The Hidden Words of Bahá'u'lláh* (Persian), no. 70.

33. *The Hidden Words of Bahá'u'lláh* (Persian), no. 75.

34. *The Hidden Words of Bahá'u'lláh* (Arabic), no. 6.

35. *The Hidden Words of Bahá'u'lláh* (Arabic), no. 23.

36. *The Hidden Words of Bahá'u'lláh* (Arabic), no. 33.

37. *The Hidden Words of Bahá'u'lláh* (Arabic), no. 34.

38. *The Hidden Words of Bahá'u'lláh* (Arabic), no. 35.

39. *The Hidden Words of Bahá'u'lláh* (Arabic), no. 63.

40. *The Hidden Words of Bahá'u'lláh* (Persian), no. 29.

41. *The Hidden Words of Bahá'u'lláh* (Persian), no. 39.

42. *The Hidden Words of Bahá'u'lláh* (Persian), no. 73.

43. *Gleanings from the Writings of Bahá'u'lláh*, pp. 132-133.

44. *Synopsis and Codification of the Laws and Ordinances of the Kitáb-i-Aqdas*, p. 15.

45. *Gleanings from the Writings of Bahá'u'lláh*, pp. 135-136.

46. *Gleanings from the Writings of Bahá'u'lláh*, p. 210.

47. *Gleanings from the Writings of Bahá'u'lláh*, p. 139.

48. *Gleanings from the Writings of Bahá'u'lláh*, p. 236.

49. *Gleanings from the Writings of Bahá'u'lláh*, p. 251.

50. *Gleanings from the Writings of Bahá'u'lláh*, p. 247.

51. *Tablets of Bahá'u'lláh*, p. 258.

52. *Tablets of Bahá'u'lláh*, p. 267.

53. *Gleanings from the Writings of Bahá'u'lláh*, p. 321.

54. *Gleanings from the Writings of Bahá'u'lláh*, pp. 328-329.

55. *Epistle to the Son of the Wolf*, p. 56.

56. *Gleanings from the Writings of Bahá'u'lláh*, pp. 127-128.

57. *Gleanings from the Writings of Bahá'u'lláh*, p. 261.

58. *The Kitáb-i-Aqdas*, 1992, p. 48.

59. *Gleanings from the Writings of Bahá'u'lláh*, p. 304-305.

60. *Kitáb-i-Íqán*, pp. 120-121.

61. *Gleanings from the Writings of Bahá'u'lláh*, pp. 138-139.

62. *The Kitáb-i-Aqdas*, 1992, pp. 44-45.

63. *Tablets of Bahá'u'lláh*, p. 232.

64. *Gleanings from the Writings of Bahá'u'lláh*, p. 126.

65. *The Kitáb-i-Aqdas*, 1992, p. 73.

66. *Tablets of Bahá'u'lláh*, pp. 265-266.
67. *Gleanings from the Writings of Bahá'u'lláh*, pp. 307-308.
68. *The Kitáb-i-Aqdas*, 1992, p. 55.
69. *Kitáb-i-Íqán*, p. 90.
70. *Synopsis and Codification of the Laws and Ordinances of the Kitáb-i-Aqdas*, p. 25.
71. *Gleanings from the Writings of Bahá'u'lláh*, p. 32.
72. *Gleanings from the Writings of Bahá'u'lláh*, p. 169.

Part II

1. *Selections from the Writings of the Báb*, p. 153.
2. *Selections from the Writings of the Báb*, p. 79.
3. *Selections from the Writings of the Báb*, p. 87.
4. *Selections from the Writings of the Báb*, p. 77.
5. *Selections from the Writings of the Báb*, pp. 88-89.
6. *Selections from the Writings of the Báb*, p. 158.
7. *Selections from the Writings of the Báb*, p. 78.
8. *Selections from the Writings of the Báb*, pp. 106-107.
9. *Selections from the Writings of the Báb*, p. 95.
10. *Selections from the Writings of the Báb*, p. 161.
11. *Selections from the Writings of the Báb*, p. 48.
12. *Selections from the Writings of the Báb*, p. 153.
13. *Selections from the Writings of the Báb*, p. 157.
14. *Selections from the Writings of the Báb*, p. 162.
15. *Selections from the Writings of the Báb*, p. 145.
16. *Selections from the Writings of the Báb*, pp. 62-63.
17. *Selections from the Writings of the Báb*, p. 163.
18. *Selections from the Writings of the Báb*, p. 52.
19. *Selections from the Writings of the Báb*, p. 50.
20. *Selections from the Writings of the Báb*, p. 67.

21. *Selections from the Writings of the Báb*, p. 157.

22. *The Seven Valleys and the Four Valleys*, p. 36.

Part III

1. *Paris Talks*, p. 85.

2. *Paris Talks*, p. 25.

3. *Paris Talks*, p. 17.

4. *Bahá'í World Faith*, p. 367.

5. *Some Answered Questions*, 1981 ed., pp. 195-196.

6. *Some Answered Questions*, 1981 ed., pp. 235-237.

7. *Some Answered Questions*, 1981 ed., pp. 233-234.

8. *Paris Talks*, pp. 66-67.

9. Goodall, Helen S., and Ella Goodall Cooper. *Daily Lessons Received At 'Akká*, Wilmette, IL: Bahá'í Publishing Trust, 1979, p. 80.

10. *Paris Talks*, pp. 88-90.

11. *Some Answered Questions*, 1981 ed., pp. 231-232.

12. *Some Answered Questions*, 1981 ed., pp. 231-232.

13. *Some Answered Questions*, 1981 ed., p. 240.

14. *Some Answered Questions*, 1981 ed., pp. 230-231.

15. *Paris Talks*, p. 178.

16. *Bahá'í World Faith*, p. 382.

17. *Selections from the Writings of 'Abdu'l-Bahá*, pp. 189-190.

18. Goodall, Helen S., and Ella Goodall Cooper. *Daily Lessons Received At 'Akká*, Wilmette, IL: Bahá'í Publishing Trust, 1979, p. 82.

19. *The Secret of Divine Civilization*, p. 19.

20. *Selections from the Writings of 'Abdu'l-Bahá*, p. 192.

21. *Some Answered Questions*, 1981 ed., p. 231.

22. *Selections from the Writings of 'Abdu'l-Bahá*, p. 191.

23. *Selections from the Writings of 'Abdu'l-Bahá*, p. 195.

24. Grundy, Julia M. *Ten Days in the Light of 'Akká*, Wilmette, IL: Bahá'í Publishing Trust, 1979, p. 41.

25. *Some Answered Questions*, 1981 ed., pp. 241-243.

26. *The Promulgation of Universal Peace*, pp. 225-227.

27. Esslemont, J.E. *Bahá'u'lláh and the New Era*, Wilmette: Bahá'í Publishing Trust, 1970, p. 190.

28. *Bahá'í World Faith*, p. 367.

29. *Selections from the Writings of 'Abdu'l-Bahá*, pp. 169-170.

30. *Selections from the Writings of 'Abdu'l-Bahá*, pp. 170-171.

31. *Selections from the Writings of 'Abdu'l-Bahá*, p. 177.

32. Esslemont, J.E. *Bahá'u'lláh and the New Era*, Wilmette: Bahá'í Publishing Trust, 1970, p. 193.

33. *Paris Talks*, p. 179.

34. Goodall, Helen S., and Ella Goodall Cooper. *Daily Lessons Received At 'Akká*, Wilmette, IL: Bahá'í Publishing Trust, 1979, pp. 78-80.

35. *Some Answered Questions*, 1981 ed., pp. 251-253.

36. Goodall, Helen S., and Ella Goodall Cooper. *Daily Lessons Received At 'Akká*, Wilmette, IL: Bahá'í Publishing Trust, 1979, p. 85.

37. *'Abdu'l-Bahá in London*, 1982, p. 96.

38. Goodall, Helen S., and Ella Goodall Cooper. *Daily Lessons Received At 'Akká*, Wilmette, IL: Bahá'í Publishing Trust, 1979, p. 82.

39. *Selections from the Writings of 'Abdu'l-Bahá*, pp. 160-161.

40. Goodall, Helen S., and Ella Goodall Cooper. *Daily Lessons Received At 'Akká*, Wilmette, IL: Bahá'í Publishing Trust, 1979, p. 78.

41. *'Abdu'l-Bahá in London*, 1982, p. 96.

42. *Selections from the Writings of 'Abdu'l-Bahá*, pp. 194-195.

43. *Selections from the Writings of 'Abdu'l-Bahá*, p. 202.

44. Esslemont, J.E. *Bahá'u'lláh and the New Era*, Wilmette: Bahá'í Publishing Trust, 1970, p. 195.

45. Esslemont, J.E. *Bahá'u'lláh and the New Era*, Wilmette: Bahá'í Publishing Trust, 1970, p. 194.

46. *A Fortress for Well-Being*, Wilmette, IL: Bahá'í Publishing Trust, 1974, p. 72.

47. *Bahá'í World Faith*, p. 372.

48. *Bahá'í World Faith*, p. 367.

49. *Some Answered Questions*, 1981 ed., p. 240.

50. Hatcher, John S. *The purpose of Physical Reality*, Wilmette, IL: Bahá'í Publishing Trust, p. 109.

51. *Selections from the Writings of 'Abdu'l-Bahá*, pp. 193-194.

52. *Selections from the Writings of 'Abdu'l-Bahá*, p. 190.

53. *'Abdu'l-Bahá in London*, 1982, p. 97.

54. *Selections from the Writings of 'Abdu'l-Bahá*, p. 81.

55. *Some Answered Questions*, 1981 ed., pp. 223-225.

56. Goodall, Helen S., and Ella Goodall Cooper. *Daily Lessons Received At 'Akká*, Wilmette, IL: Bahá'í Publishing Trust, 1979, pp. 81-82.

57. *Selections from the Writings of 'Abdu'l-Bahá*, p. 194.

58. *Selections from the Writings of 'Abdu'l-Bahá*, p. 194.

59. *Selections from the Writings of 'Abdu'l-Bahá*, pp. 64-65.

60. *The Promulgation of Universal Peace*, pp. 46-48.

61. *Selections from the Writings of 'Abdu'l-Bahá*, pp. 199-200.

62. *Selections from the Writings of 'Abdu'l-Bahá*, pp. 187-189.

63. *Selections from the Writings of 'Abdu'l-Bahá*, p. 197.

64. *Selections from the Writings of 'Abdu'l-Bahá*, pp. 200-201.

65. *Selections from the Writings of 'Abdu'l-Bahá*, p. 201.

66. *Memorials of the Faithful*, p. 12.

67. *The Secret of Divine Civilization*, pp. 102-103.

68. *Bahá'í World Faith*, pp. 370-371.

69. *Selections from the Writings of 'Abdu'l-Bahá*, pp. 183-184.

70. *Some Answered Questions*, 1981 ed., pp. 282-289.

71. *Some Answered Questions*, 1981 ed., pp. 143-145.

72. *Some Answered Questions,* 1981 ed., pp. 198-199.

73. *Some Answered Questions,* 1981 ed., pp. 151-152.

74. *Some Answered Questions,* 1981 ed., pp. 200-201.

75. *The Promulgation of Universal Peace,* pp. 294-296.

76. *Some Answered Questions,* 1981 ed., pp. 205-207.

77. *Paris Talks,* pp. 96-99.

78. *Some Answered Questions,* 1981 ed., pp. 208-209.

79. *Paris Talks,* pp. 64-66.

80. *Some Answered Questions,* 1981 ed., pp. 239-240.

81. *Paris Talks,* pp. 86-87.

82. *Bahá'í World Faith,* pp. 337-338.

83. *Bahá'í World Faith,* pp. 346-347.

84. *Foundations of World Unity,* pp. 109-110.

85. *The Promulgation of Universal Peace,* pp. 240-243.

86. *Some Answered Questions,* 1981 ed., pp. 185-190.

87. *'Abdu'l-Bahá in London,* 1982, p. 97.

88. *Paris Talks,* pp. 90-94.

89. *Some Answered Questions,* 1981 ed., pp. 225-226.

90. *Some Answered Questions,* 1981 ed., pp. 227-229.

91. Grundy, Julia M. *Ten Days in the Light of 'Akká,* Wilmette, IL: Bahá'í Publishing Trust, 1979, p. 77.

92. *Bahá'í World Faith,* pp. 340-341.

93. Maxwell, May. *An Early Pilgrimage,* London: George Ronald, 1953, p. 28.

94. *'Abdu'l-Bahá in London,* 1982, pp. 95-96.

95. *Selections from the Writings of 'Abdu'l-Bahá,* p. 204-205.

96. *Selections from the Writings of 'Abdu'l-Bahá,* p. 204.

97. *Tablets of the Divine Plan,* p. 73.

98. *Selections from the Writings of 'Abdu'l-Bahá,* pp. 177-178.

99. *Selections from the Writings of 'Abdu'l-Bahá,* pp. 184-185.

100. Shoghi Effendi. *The Dispensation of Bahá'u'lláh,* Wilmette, IL: Bahá'í Publishing Committee, 1947, pp. 18-19.

101. *Selections from the Writings of 'Abdu'l-Bahá*, p. 186.

102. Maxwell, May. *An Early Pilgrimage*, London: George Ronald, 1953, pp. 26-27.

103. *Selections from the Writings of 'Abdu'l-Bahá*, pp. 220-221.

Part IV

1. *Prayers and Meditations by Bahá'u'lláh*, pp. 260-261.

2. *Synopsis and Codification of the Laws and Ordinances of the Kitáb-i-Aqdas*, p. 58.

3. *Synopsis and Codification of the Laws and Ordinances of the Kitáb-i-Aqdas*, p. 62.

4. *Bahá'í Prayers*, Wilmette, IL: Bahá'í Publishing Trust, 1991 ed., pp. 41-42.

5. *Gleanings from the Writings of Bahá'u'lláh*, pp. 133-134.

6. *Bahá'í Prayers*, Wilmette, IL: Bahá'í Publishing Trust, 1991 ed., pp. 43-45.

7. *Selections from the Writings of the Báb*, pp. 203-204.

8. *Selections from the Writings of the Báb*, p. 177.

9. *Selections from the Writings of the Báb*, p. 210.

10. *Selections from the Writings of the Báb*, p. 182.

11. *Selections from the Writings of the Báb*, p. 178.

12. *Selections from the Writings of the Báb*, p. 177.

13. *Bahá'í Prayers*, Wilmette, IL: Bahá'í Publishing Trust, 1991 ed., pp. 45-46.

14. *Bahá'í Prayers*, Wilmette, IL: Bahá'í Publishing Trust, 1991 ed., pp. 46-47.

Part V

1. *Epistle to the Son of the Wolf*, p. 112.

Index

W

Y

Sources for Information and Literature

If you wish to receive further information on the Bahá'í Faith please write to:

Alaska
Alaska Book Committee
13501 Brayton Drive
Anchorage, Alaska 99516

Australia
Bahá'í Publications
P.O. Box 285
Mona Vale, N.S.W. 2103
Australia

Canada
Bahá'í National Centre
7200 Leslie Street
Thornhill, Ontario
L3T 6L8 Canada

Great Britain

Bahá'í Publishing Trust of the
United Kingdom
6 Mount Pleasant
Oakham, Leicestshire
LEI5 6HU England

Hawaiian Islands

National Spiritual Assembly of the
Bahá'ís of the Hawaiian Islands
3264 Allan Place
Honolulu, Hawaii 96817

New Zealand

National Spiritual Assembly of
Bahá'ís of New Zealand
Bahá'í National Office
P.O. Box 21-551
Henderson 1231
Auckland
New Zealand

United States

Bahá'í National Center
Wilmette, Illinois 60091
USA

I Shall Come Again

- *A book addressed to Christians to prove that they need not wait any longer for the return of their Redeemer, that the promise of Christ's return has already been fulfilled!*

- *The culmination of over two decades of research.*

- *A challenging, comprehensive, and thoroughly documented work on the proofs of Bahá'u'lláh's Mission.*

A book with a message of hope and fulfillment, a message that can transform our planet into a place of peace, into a kingdom that has been the dream and hope of humanity since the dawn of history...a scholarly, comprehensive, and fascinating work that has been long overdue. No wonder it took over two decades to complete it. **Hon. Dorothy W. Nelson, D.J.**
Judge, Court of Appeals, 9th circuit

This book says that the Epiphany is now...that it is not yet too late to join in the Sacred Ritual that presages the redemption of man. In love there is no threat. This book, like all sacred scholarship, is an act of love. It is also an act of scholarship. **William Maxwell, Ed.D.**
Chairman, The IQ Foundation

Your work is the best I've seen on biblical prophecies and proofs of Bahá'u'lláh's Revelation. You offer so much information in relatively few pages. Your many references prove clearly the book's central claim. Your language is simple and exciting. You take the reader through a complete spiritual and prophetic adventure. Your approach is modest, yet dynamic. I pray it will excite all your readers as it has excited me. **J. Killeen**
Bible scholar, with a degree in eschatology and soteriology

An important work that will be referenced by future Bahá'í scholars for millennia to come. **Robert F. Riggs**
Aerospace and Marine Scientist, Inventor, Author of *The Apocalypse Unsealed*

A unique feature of *I Shall Come Again,* and the four volumes that follow it, is the application of statistical probabilities to the fulfillment of prophecies. In Volume II (*Lord of Lords and King of Kings*), the author applies the basic laws of chance to prophecies of both the first and second advents of Christ. He shows that the odds against chance in both advents are astronomical. The odds against chance in the first advent are calculated by two Christian scholars (Newman and Stoner) to be 10^{17}. The odds against chance in the second advent are calculated by Dr. Motlagh to be 4×10^{94}. That is equal to 4×10^{17} times the number of elementary particles (electrons, protons, and neutrons) in the known universe! As you can see, a comparison between the two figures shows that on the basis of prophecies, the proof of the second advent, compared to the first, is stronger by as many times as there are elementary particles in the known universe!

I Shall Come Again

Volume I
Time Prophecies

Husbidar Motlagh, Ed.D.

Foreword by the Hon.
Dorothy W. Nelson,
Judge, U.S. Court of Appeals

Global Perspective

―――――――✂―――――――

Please send me _____ copies of *I Shall Come Again, Volume I,* (484 pages), softcover at $25.00, hardcover at $35.00.

☐ Check enclosed, made payable to *Global Perspective,*

for _____.

☐ Charge my ☐ VISA ☐ Mastercard

Card number _____

Expiration date _____

Signature _____

Send book to:
Name: (print) _____

Address: (print) _____

City/State/Zip: (print) _____

Phone: (_____) _____
Mail to: *Global Perspective,* 1106 Greenbanks Dr., Mt. Pleasant, Michigan 48858, USA